"Fashioned as a handbook for spiritual mentors, this book offers so much more depth and discernment than simple instruction. It has more the feel of an artisan teaching their craft than a technician explaining a manual. Poetic and deeply humanizing with story, metaphor, and cultural memory, Dr. Anderson invites spiritual mentors to listen to the life stories of their mentees as narratives cowritten with God. He reminds us that listening to God and being listened to are not competing ends. We are not calling people to a discipline of self negation, but towards a refocus on God as the center of their efforts to know themselves. This text assumes a posture of relatedness and reveals the necessary interplay of the human and divine embrace, 'God is with us and we are not alone.' Dr. Anderson's integrative thinking and thoughtful use of the his own narrative make this a rare and worthy offering."

J. Derek McNeil, senior vice president of academics, The Seattle School of Theology and Psychology

"Since first meeting Keith Anderson I knew he was a man of many talents and virtues. As I have gotten to know him more I would say that his greatest virtue is curiosity, and I mean that as the highest compliment. *Reading Your Life's Story* shares this tremendous virtue of his so that we might be more curious, both about our own lives and about the lives we are so blessedly honored and called to mentor. In my visits with him I have been blessed to be the recipient of his mentoring and therefore can speak to the mastery he humbly shares in this book. This is an excellent book on a topic we desperately need to know about—and practice—more."

Gregory H. Rickel, eighth bishop of Olympia

"*Reading Your Life's Story* is everything and much more than the author is willing to claim, offering relevant, timeless insights into a vitally essential kind of friendship. Keith Anderson understands that discovering our life's story is a spiritual journey that we must not embark on alone. Like its author, this luminous, thoughtful book is filled with wisdom, grace, and truth, reminding readers that those who fail to know their life's story risk creating a breach between what they believe and how they live."

Fil Anderson, pastor, spiritual director, author of *Running on Empty*

"For anyone seeking wisdom on how to navigate being a spiritual mentor, *Reading Your Life's Story* is an amazing place to start. Furthermore, it offers incredible gems for anyone who wants to be a better witness to others."

Naomi Wachira, Afro-Folk singer-songwriter

"A practical guide to spiritual mentoring for normal people! In *Reading Your Life's Story*, Keith Anderson equips the amateur and veteran mentor alike to help people pay attention to the work of God in their lives. I can't wait to use it at my university and in my church."

Rod Reed, dean of Christian formation at John Brown University, coeditor of *Building a Culture of Faith*

"By applying the art and science of mentoring relationships to the canvas of spiritual formation, Keith Anderson invites us to see and hear, through the senses and heart of listener and reader, the story that God is writing in each life. Keith understands that spiritual mentoring brings mentor and mentee into the presence of God at work in both lives—two people observing together the movement of the Spirit around them. This important book invites, inspires, and instructs mentor and mentee alike."

Walter C. Wright Jr., senior fellow, Max De Pree Center for Leadership, author of *Relational Leadership* and *The Third Third of Life*

Reading Your Life's Story

An Invitation to Spiritual Mentoring

Keith R. Anderson

IVP Books

An imprint of InterVarsity Press
Downers Grove, Illinois

InterVarsity Press
P.O. Box 1400, Downers Grove, IL 60515-1426
ivpress.com
email@ivpress.com

InterVarsity Press® is the book-publishing division of InterVarsity Christian Fellowship/USA®, a movement of students and faculty active on campus at hundreds of universities, colleges and schools of nursing in the United States of America, and a member movement of the International Fellowship of Evangelical Students. For information about local and regional activities, visit intervarsity.org.

Scripture quotations, unless otherwise noted, are from the New Revised Standard Version of the Bible, copyright 1989 by the Division of Christian Education of the National Council of the Churches of Christ in the USA. Used by permission. All rights reserved.

The song on pp. 145–46 is Holy as a Day is Spent, lyrics courtesy of Carrie Newcomer © 2002 Carrie Newcomer Music, admin. BMG/Chrysalis.

While any stories in this book are true, some names and identifying information may have been changed to protect the privacy of individuals.

Cover design: Cindy Kiple
Interior design: Beth McGill
Images: ©Bill Reitzel/Getty Images

ISBN 978-0-8308-4621-4 (print)
ISBN 978-0-8308-7319-7 (digital)

Printed in the United States of America ∞

Library of Congress Cataloging-in-Publication Data
A catalog record for this book is available from the Library of Congress.

P 25 24 23 22 21 20 19 18 17 16 15 14 13 12 11 10 9 8 7 6 5 4 3 2 1

Y 34 33 32 31 30 29 28 27 26 25 24 23 22 21 20 19 18 17 16

With profound thanks for the entire great cloud of witnesses,
especially Doc Dalton, Garth Rosell and Dan Erwin:
you got me started.

And Brennan Manning: you helped me find my way back.

Contents

Introduction

Mentoring Matters

*The books the Holy Spirit is writing are living,
and every soul a volume in which the divine author
makes a true revelation of his word, explaining it to
every heart, unfolding it in every moment.*

JEAN-PIERRE DE CAUSSADE

The day started as others before had for the college student. He ate breakfast standing at the counter, gathered books and note-books, drove to campus, walked hurriedly to the classroom building, and then it happened. Papers were returned with bright red comments and grades crisscrossing the pages, and his had a note that said something unexpected: "Excellent thinking! A." I was that student, and for the first time in my life, a trusted teacher recognized my work and, more importantly, told me so. That afternoon, I went to him and the unexpected happened again. He said to me, "I would like to meet with you periodically to talk about your academic work." The invitation was startling but welcome. It began what turned into a long relationship of professor and student, friend and friend, mentor and mentee. I didn't know then what a mentor was, but I was eager for the afternoons to meet with Dr. Rosell for conversation. His questions weren't complex but rather ordinary and provocative in their simplicity: "What have you been working on? What are you thinking about? What are you reading that interests you?" The questions weren't as important as the invitation. The conversation wasn't even as important as the authentic curiosity it expressed. I was changing from an underachieving student into a "scholar" or, as I fancied, an "intellectual." He didn't seek me out for my intellectually stimulating questions, of that I am sure. Instead, he seemed to see something in me that he believed had value, and he nurtured a soaring sense of *agency* in me, a deep recognition that I was someone to be valued and heard. That changed me.

There is a singular human need common to us all. Because we are created in the *imago Dei*, in the image of the trinitarian God who is, by nature, relational, we share a universal human need for relationship. There is no solitary individual; we are persons, by our very nature created for relationship. Biblical text is clear from the beginning: God calls us into relationship. Telling our story and being heard is a human need common to us all. To be human is to tell one's story to another. Narrative is the essential form of human speech. We tell each other the ordinary story of our day or the extraordinary story of an epic event, but we need others in our life who care to listen. My grandchildren are moving from the earliest form of narrative, "Read me a story, Papa" or "Tell me a story" to "Let me tell *you* a story, Papa." Two ears for listening, one voice for speaking—we understand the mathematics of our human anatomy—but we have one heart and soul that doesn't just long for conversation but needs to be heard by others. Telling our story is to our spirit what the flow of blood is to our body.

- True to our relational nature, we are created for dialogical speech.

- True to our spirituality, we yearn to live our stories aware of the presence of God.

- True to our psychological nature, we seek the bond of human recognition and human touch.

- True to our communal makeup, we need human companionship.

- True to our emotional character, we desire trusted intimacy.

- True to our kinship character, we are naturally drawn to be storytellers with others.

- True to our created nature, we are created to reveal our spirit to others through story.

Storytelling is an essential act of human friendship. Early in the world of Roman philosophical thought, Cicero penned a classic dissertation on the nature of human friendship. In *De Amicitia*, he asserted that, except for wisdom, friendship is the greatest gift given to humankind. He pondered the advantages of friendship and wondered aloud if it arises from weakness but concluded, "Wherefore it seems to me that friendship springs rather from nature than from need, and from an inclination of the soul joined with a feeling of love rather than from calculation of how much profit the friendship is likely to afford."[1] In his text he describes the ideal location and purpose to gather friends: it is a garden setting with a semicircle of chairs as a gathering place with a wise friend and "only a few of his intimate friends."[2] What would be the topic of conversation for such discourse? Cicero's answer is decisive: "What is sweeter than to have someone with whom you may dare discuss anything as if you were communing with yourself? . . . Friendship embraces innumerable ends; turn where you will it is ever at your side; no barrier shuts it out; it is never untimely and never in the way."[3]

As Jesus prepared to leave his students behind, he no doubt startled them with what may be his most unexpected words. After many months with his student-disciples, he declared, "I do not call you servants any longer, because the servant does not know what the master is doing; but I have called you friends, because I have made known to you everything that I have heard from my Father" (John 15:15). The relationship transformed from that of student or disciple to friendship. Remarkable. Jesus offered friendship to his students. A new kind of companionship had been formed—the functional relationship of teacher-student converted to friendship. Still their teacher, still their rabbi, still their Lord, but now also their friend, companion and trusted confidant ("I have made known to you everything that I have heard from my Father.") I opened an email from such a friend who I haven't seen in some months and read his heart through his tender words, "I am eager to be in the room with you as well. Look you in the eye, and tell you I love you."

The book you hold in your hand is about a particular kind of friendship called spiritual mentoring. It is a particular kind of companionship in which two or more people walk together in heightened awareness of the presence of yet another, the Holy Spirit, who is the living presence of God promised by Jesus who said, "Remember, I am with you always, to the end of the age" (Matthew 28:20). Spiritual mentoring is not a complicated process requiring technical training and complex protocol. It is essential, authentic and maybe even natural human speech that is focused, disciplined and nurtured by training for one of the hardest things we do: listening reflectively to another. It is sacred companionship as life is lived and story told. Available to almost all, mentoring requires deliberate recruitment, preparation and practice. One of our wisest spiritual teachers today, Eugene Peterson, said, "The way of Jesus cannot be imposed or mapped—it requires an active participation in following Jesus as he leads us through sometimes strange and unfamiliar territory, in circumstances that become clear only in the hesitations and questionings, in the pauses and reflections where we engage in prayerful conversation with one another and with him."[4]

WHAT THIS BOOK IS ABOUT

I struggle to call this book a handbook, but it offers insights that can be used by a first-time mentor. I hesitate to call it a guide, because the true guide for all spirituality is the Holy Spirit; this book merely points us to the Spirit. In my ministry and work I have taught courses, seminars and conferences on spiritual mentoring. I am always most comfortable speaking of my work primarily as an *introduction* to spiritual mentoring because it seems to me that all of our work in spirituality is only that—an introduction, a handshake and a brief encounter. Just as a topographical map does not contain the experience of trekking, hiking or mountain climbing, so this book cannot capture the deeply sacred work of spiritual mentoring. It would be arrogant to say otherwise. Even an entire course on spiritual mentoring only offers a prelude to this richly nuanced work, but it can offer enough for one to get started. This volume is an invitation to learn to read your life as story in the companionship of spiritual friendship and to come alongside others to read their life as story. Whether you are mentor or mentee, the task is the same: you learn to read life as story and invite others into prayerful conversation; it is an invitation.

A spiritual mentor is anyone who guides us in our spiritual formation. Some guidance occurs naturally in the shared life of good friends, and there is great value in this. But there is a distinctive form of guidance in the steps taken intentionally as part of relationships with spiritual directors, mentors and spiritual friends. Common to all of these relationships is a mutual commitment to spiritual growth. Whether old or young, living or dead, ancient or contemporary, known personally or from afar by reading or listening, spiritual mentors are guides. They point the way. They offer their experience of the journey. They help us read the story well, to see what we might otherwise miss. Story is meant to be read in companionship and in the presence of the Holy Spirit. Jesus' parting promise to his followers was that the Spirit would come to his disciples after his ascension into heaven. Instructions were given "through the Holy Spirit to the apostles" (Acts 1:2) in the early hours after the resurrection. It was only the beginning of the companionship intended for all flesh, sons and daughters, young men and old men on whom God promised to pour out God's own Spirit (Acts 2:17-18).

There are many who provide spiritual guidance. In this book, however, the invitation is to mentoring as an intentional, planned, repeated and focused set of conversations about the life of the mentee in the presence of the Holy Spirit. It is not the same as the classical, hierarchical style of *spiritual direction*, and it is more than the spontaneous conversations of *spiritual friendship*. And yet, while the practices discussed in coming chapters refer to this particular form of ministry called spiritual mentoring, the skills, intuitions and instincts can also be useful for spiritual directors and spiritual friends. Much is made of the differences between these forms of spiritual formation, but I believe we are best helped by gleaning wisdom from all sources rather than emphasizing the differences between them.

My life has been touched by spiritual directors, mentors and guides in formal and informal ways. Some are people I've never met except as I've listened to their voices in their writings; they have taught me to listen, see and read more fully what I cannot read as well on my own—the still, small voice of God's Holy Spirit. Some of my best mentors have been people dead for centuries, whose texts, prayers, sermons, poetry, art and stories have served as guides, correctives and shaping voices to me because their voices are animated still. Brother Lawrence, Teresa of Ávila, Thomas á Kempis, Julian of Norwich, Richard Baxter, John of the Cross, Ignatius of Loyola, Catherine of Siena, Jeanne Guyon, John Calvin and Simone Weil are some whose words have touched my life. There are other, more contemporary guides known to me through conversation or reading, such as Henri Nouwen, Brennan Manning, Eugene Peterson, James Houston, Frederick Buechner, Annie Dillard, Wendell Berry and Barbara Brown Taylor. Some have been friends, colleagues, brothers and sisters with whom I have shared life and ministry. A large group includes students and mentees who I have been privileged to know, many of whom I now consider my mentors—Rod, Linda, Guy, JP, Trygve, Tom, David, Steve and dozens of others. My mentors have included a woman trained at Church of the Savior in Washington, DC, a Jesuit priest trained in Ignatian practices, a Baptist minister trained in psychology and pastoral care, a seminary president, a university president and pastor, a de-frocked Catholic priest, writer and spiritual teacher, and a multitude of Benedictine sisters trained in abbeys as nuns. And finally, some are the voices of family, especially the one I am most blessed to spend my life with—the most important voice in my world—Wendy Lee McJunkin Anderson.

READING ON PURPOSE

This book is about a specific kind of mentoring in which there is an intentional companionship of listening together to the living voice of the Holy Spirit in the text of one's life. Much of what I am writing can apply to life's many forms of friendship mentoring and the mentoring that comes from books, occasional conversations or casual discourse, and shared meals, but my focus here is on spiritual mentoring as a specific and disciplined form of one individual guiding another in the presence of the Holy Spirit. It is what I have come to think of as learning to read one's story in companionship with the Holy Spirit on purpose.

The metaphor of mentoring as reading story acknowledges three essential factors: author, reader(s) and text.

First, there is an author who intends to do something in the writing of the book. He or she is not merely writing a collection of words; in good writing an author has something purposeful in mind—entertainment, biography, science, comedy, tragedy, fiction or fairy tale—there is intentionality. In good stories, the author is usually unnoticed in the background because you are caught up in the story. At times, however, the author may be in front of you, figuratively, as you ask, "What is the point? Where is she taking me in this twisted turn? What does he think he's doing by the introduction of this character?" Loud or quiet, visible or not, the author is a partner in reading the story. God is writing our story in providential moments of our lives.

Second, there is a reader, or multiple readers, ready to engage the work of the author. There are many ways to read, possibly as many ways as there are readers. But good reading involves a spirit of curiosity on the part of a reader. The page-turner that you can't put down keeps you waiting, almost breathless, to see what happens next as you turn the page to the next chapter. Poetry might be read slowly, reflectively and repeatedly. You ponder and wonder what meaning is implied or captured in the imagery and vocabulary of the poem on the page. Technical reading may be done as study with a dictionary, other texts for comparison and another reader who can help you see the author's design. Reading with a young child requires stops along the way to laugh, learn the meaning of words, puzzle over the plot or just enjoy the story as it unfolds in the imagination of the reader. In biblical studies, we use the word *exegesis* to describe the process of reading. On a quest to discover meaning in the text, hermeneutics help us notice literary type, vocabulary, sentence structure, context and what we bring to the text by way of interpreter's bias, assumptions and perspective. Regardless of the type of text, readers bring one essential skill to any kind of reading: curiosity. A mentee is the primary reader, but the mentor becomes a coreader whose questions, insights and musings help the mentee read his or her own story with more evocative thought and sometimes with greater clarity.

Finally, there is a text. I know that sounds obvious, but it needs to be said. Reading is rooted in a text. There are words on a page that you will learn to take seriously if you proceed reading. There is content, in other words, that comes in specific words and a particular form. In this metaphor, your life story is the text that has shape, specificity, design, vocabulary and progression of thought. The text sets boundaries in place that limit what it says and, therefore, what it means. If the text is a life, reading requires careful, respectful engagement. Reading, it turns out, is a holy task. Reading a story engages the mind (body) but also emotions, relationships and the soul. Reading is anything but passive; it engages the whole person. Reading life as a story is a way of relational engagement with a sacred purpose. The text I'm talking about includes all parts of life; that cannot be overstated. The text is not just some selected so-called spiritual moments; all of life is text to read.

It's more than a poetic metaphor; if I see my life as story, I am moved to read it with curious eyes. I *read* my life as precious and sacred. I look for signs of the author's pen in events and moments. I ask better questions than "How was your day?" or "What did you do on your vacation?" If I see my life as story, I know it to be an invitation to enter the great adventure, battle and drama of the unfolding narrative of my life in a world that is inhabited with the presence and voice of God.

If you have picked up this book you are looking for something to help you become either a mentor for others or to be mentored yourself. The answer is not far off but within. Thomas Kelley was a Quaker, teacher, writer and philosopher who described what he called an inner sanctuary of the soul. It is a living place, a dynamic center where God's voice may be heard. He declared it *shekinah*, the Hebrew word for dwelling or settling, an experience of the very presence of God grounded in the soil of life. His image of the inner sanctuary is how I imagine my work as a mentor. I join the mentee in a holy place as we find the voice and face of God waiting to be revealed.

> Deep within us all there is an amazing inner sanctuary of the soul, a holy place, a Divine Center, a speaking Voice to which we may continuously return. Eternity is at our hearts, pressing upon our time-worn lives, warming us with intimations of an astounding destiny, calling us home unto itself. Yielding to these persuasions, gladly committing ourselves in body and soul, utterly and complete, to the Light Within, is the beginning of true life. It is a dynamic center, a creative Life that presses to birth within us. It is a Light Within which illuminates the face of God and casts new shadows and new glories upon the face of men [and women]. It is a seed stirring to life if we do not choke it. It is the Shekinah of the soul, the Presence in the midst.[5]

This is where I believe we go to uncover the story of the mentee.

Part One

Uncovering Your Life Story

1

Reading with a
Consecrated Purpose

Learning to read was both natural and easy for me as a young child. Words became like pictures that offered a portal into a world of color, beauty, imagery and a strange kind of power. Yes, the ability to interpret the meaning of the lines on a page was power, even for a small boy. By second grade I loved words even more because they had moved from simple vocabulary to story. They had become a direct doorway into imagination. The Hardy Boys mysteries, the Sugar Creek Gang and other stories acceptable in my Christian home became frequent companions at night under the covers with a smuggled flashlight but also outside on a summer's day or in the private world of boyhood imagination. Books from school were allowed, so I read *To Kill a Mockingbird*, *Black Like Me* and *The Red Badge of Courage*. At home we also listened to stories on the radio—missionary drama and rescue from addiction on the mean streets of the cities. Of course, the constant companion in my family was the Bible, with its stories of women and men of faith, courage, conviction and obedience. Only later did I discover these people also had stories of disobedience, fear, deception and failure. Later also came my "intellectual period" with Russian writers Solzhenitsyn, Dostoyevsky and Tolstoy. The Beat Poets and Ferlinghetti were companions for a time and, by contrast, so were Dag Hammarskjöld, Robert Frost, and Emily Dickinson. Now I am eager for Wendell Berry, Billy Collins, David McCullough biographies, and even pulp fiction.

At one point I traded fiction and poetry for what I deemed to be more scholarly work as I studied history, political science, theology and spirituality. But somehow my calling as pastor, teacher and preacher kept stories close. You cannot preach gospel well without story, just as you cannot live the meaning of gospel well without engaging your own story. We often say at the Seattle School of Theology and Psychology that you cannot take others farther than you have been willing to go yourself. One of our signature programs is the Story Workshop, which takes people into the crucible of learning to tell their story of tragedy to a small group. A trained facilitator is present to assist in "reading" the story well together because we believe our spirituality is shaped by narrative and how we tell the stories of our lives. Story is not only fiction or history, chronology and timeline; story is meaning making in its most formative sense. We are formed by our story and we are formed as we tell our story to others and as we learn to read our life as story *with* others. We who are mentors might be considered selfish people. We mentor others because we love story, and we read the lives of our mentees because we receive so much as we do. On our best days, we know it is about the other, but on all days we are deeply touched because we've been invited into their life.

Spiritual mentoring is learning to read *all* of their story—desire and tragedy, beauty and shame, glory and failure. It is not simply to mark change in the way we chart the upward growth of a child in pencil on a doorway in the bedroom; not simply a timeline to chart years passed, moments experienced and events undergone. In spiritual mentoring we recognize all of life as story. Mark Twain said his first rule in story writing was that "a tale should accomplish something and arrive somewhere."[1] Others point out that a story has, at least, a beginning, a middle and an end. Reading a story, then, starts with an understanding of how a story actually "works."

THE ELEMENTS OF HOLY NARRATIVE

What are the elements of a story? At its simplest, there are at least five elements of a story.

- There is an author.

- There is an unfolding plot, a theme, question or issue that gives coherence to the story. In classical stories this may be the conflict that initiates the story.

- There are characters.

- There are events, ordinary and surprising, that form the backbone of the story in context as the plot develops.

- There may be a resolution, climax or denouement—or not. In contemporary American fiction, a new popular form is an abrupt conclusion that only hints at how the story will actually end, but there is a movement or flow as an author narrates to a moment of conclusion.

Each of these will aid us as we learn the role of mentoring another. Reminded of authorship (authorization and authority), we will keep the focus on God's primary role in cocreating the story. Reminded of plot, we will learn to read for intentionality, themes and meaning in the seemingly random events of life. Reminded of characters, we will see development, formation, malformation, regression and surprising growth in ourselves through interaction with others. Reminded of the place of events, we will look to both the ordinary and extraordinary as formational and generative and lived in a particular context of time and place. And reminded of resolution, we will learn that there is no final telling of our story in this life but rather in eternity. Reading story as holy narrative is a nuanced metaphor for the richness, individuality and complexity of a person. It is a sacred task to be done carefully, respectfully and in holy curiosity. It is reading with a consecrated purpose.

My Life as a House is the story of a man who is dying of cancer, but only he knows his diagnosis. I've seen the movie at least a half dozen times. It draws me in by its plot but more, I suppose, by the emotions it evokes in me. He is divorced from his wife and estranged from his self-loathing and rebellious teenage son, who considers his father a relic of something long since forgotten. He owns a piece of property that overlooks the California coast that once contained a ramshackle house built by his own father. Fired by his architectural company, in a rage he destroys all of the architectural models he has created over his career but keeps the design of a house he once crafted. In an act of undetermined motivation he decides to build a new house based on the one remaining model to replace the house his father had built years before.

After his death there is a voice-over in which the architect, George, speaks to his son about his life and house. "I always thought of myself as a house. I was always what I lived in. It didn't need to be big; it didn't even need to be beautiful; it just needed to be mine. I became what I was meant to be. I built myself a life. . . . I built myself a house." Building a house was the plot for the father, George (Kevin Kline), to read the final chapter of his own unfolding story.

We live in what we have built. The stories of our life become a house we inhabit with its limitations, eccentricities, mistakes, hidden meanings and crafted beauty. In this book I hope to offer ways to help us all read the story of our life through the centuries-deep practice of spiritual mentoring. Stories are a way to find coherence and meaning in what seems random, episodic or even chaotic. Alan Jones's words are irrepressibly stunning: "My drifting is consecrated in pilgrimage"[2]

"Passion for pilgrimage," the title of Jones's book, is one way to describe our human longing for meaning. What the spiritual teachers of my life share in common, along with generations of others named and anonymous, is that they practiced spiritual friendship on a common quest for identity, community and purpose. Spiritual mentoring is not a form of evangelism, catechism or pastoral care, per se; it is an embodiment of spiritual companionship. The mentor chooses to walk alongside another in what Celtic spirituality calls *anamchara*—soul friendship—seeking to find meaning on the journey. It may be as simple as two friends who share a common hunger for faith who know they need companions for the journey. It is enriched by centuries of wisdom distilled from spiritual directors, monastics, clergy, priests, and very ordinary women and men who reached out to another to sit at the table of spiritual nurture in this ministry of reading the story of each other's lives. It is the recognition that I can be helped through the wisdom of one who has climbed this mountain trail before and is willing to sit by the fire and tell the stories of their own trek across terrain I now will walk. The book that will be read is the life story of the mentee.

Mentors are, most often, people we know who live alongside us as companions of the sacred in the most ordinary ways. Pilgrimage is a metaphor that speaks of an earlier era or a dramatic spiritual quest. Lacy Ellman is a spiritual director who once was a student of mine. She says:

> Though ancient in its roots, the practice of pilgrimage is alive and well today, beckoning a new generation of seekers to journey beyond the edge of daily life into terrains of mystery, wonder, revelation, delight, acceptance and transformation. But you don't have to leave home to begin living like a pilgrim. To live as a pilgrim at home, all you need to do is to see your life as a journey and your role as a seeker of the Sacred.[3]

Yesterday two men spoke to me at a conference with eyes glistening with joy. "You know our best friend, PJ." They were correct. I knew PJ as a student who I was privileged to spend time with frequently over his college career. "You gave him tenderness as a new follower of Jesus." That same day a woman at the conference said, "You know my pastor. She was your student." I knew immediately who she was. In both cases I lit up with anticipation to hear about their work and ministry. I was humbled to be remembered by PJ and Georgia after so many years. I tell these stories to say it is an immense privilege to be asked to walk alongside a mentee. But I remember the gift of relationship with them both. Their stories are as different as can be, but the common thread was intentional time spent learning to read each story. It is a holy vocation, this calling to mentor another. The privilege is not to be taken for granted.

WRITTEN ON LIFE BY THE SPIRIT

Long before there was a category of narrative theology there was spiritual guidance offered to princes and kings, laborers and maidservants, woman and men in agriculture, business, education, health care, and the arts. Teresa was a spiritual guide to her monastic community in Ávila, Spain. She described spirituality as a seven-room castle and said our work is to learn to open the doors and move deeper and deeper into the interior castle, which is our own soul. Richard Baxter taught his congregation in Kidderminster, England, in the seventeenth century that their mission was to spend time in each other's homes as living images of Christ to one another. He insisted on careful attention to individuals as a shepherd, schoolmaster or doctor would. At the very core of his insistence on such a particularized approach to people was a deep pastoral love for people.[4] Aelred of Rievaulx was a Cistercian monk in England in the eleventh century who wrote a remarkable book about a most ordinary topic: friendship. He said, "No medicine is more valuable, none more efficacious, none better suited to the cure of all our temporal ills than a friend to whom we may turn for consolation in time of trouble, and with whom we may share our happiness in time of joy."[5] Mentoring is holy listening in companionship—mentor, mentee and the Holy Spirit.

The apostle Paul chose the word *letter* to describe what I call "story," and his writing is startling in its clarity. He said to a congregation in Greece, "You are a *letter* of Christ, prepared by us, written not with ink but with the Spirit of the living God, not on tablets of stone but on tablets of human hearts."[6] This verse contains an entire volume of Paul's theology; the progression insists on our attention:

- Christ is the source, the originator and the one whose work in their lives comes first.

- The readers are "prepared" in *koinonia*, solidarity, partnership or mentoring by others.

- The Spirit of the living God etches God's presence on their hearts, souls and lives.

It's true that you can't love in abstraction. The grammar is straightforward: there is an object of one's love. Love is embodied in presence and voice, written "not on tablets of stone but on tablets of human hearts." The story of Jesus in a person's life is not an abstraction, concept or cognition; it is a story, a living relationship written by the Holy Spirit and embodied in those who come alongside to help "prepare" them. There are relationships all around—*inside* all parts of our story as Christ writes himself into our lives; *within* as the Spirit writes on our hearts; *alongside* as others help us read what is being written; *beyond*, to those with whom we tell the story of what has been written.

What I bring to this book is time spent in the presence of the living God with people on a shared "long walk of faith."[7] I make no claim to be a master teacher of spiritual mentoring but rather am a student of those who have shaped my faith by their faith. I make no claim to be other than I am—a failed, flawed, finite and limited human being with an endless curiosity to hear the voice of God in my story and others. For every story that can warm my heart as a mentor, I suppose there are stories where I missed the point or read or listened less well than I intended. I write to give voice to the voices I have been gifted to listen to over a lifetime. As much as anything else I will tell what I have received from gifted soul friends, mentors and mentees in my life. I write to invite you to learn to read your story in companionship with others whose accents and intonations you know well because they have already spoken into your life. I write to tell the experiences I have been privileged to have as a mentee to gifted mentors and to invite others to find someone to come alongside to help them learn to read the unfolding story of their lives. I chose the language of "learning to read" because it takes us back to a time and place of basic curiosity about "all those lines and circles"[8] on the page, the mystery of meaning contained in words. It takes us back to a place of humility as we start at step one—learning letters, then vocabulary, sentence structure, and eventually plot, character development and the flow of narrative. It takes us back to the ABCs of reading; similarly, in spirituality we are always children taking the next step.

The creed that has guided my work in pastoral life in congregations, Christian universities and theological graduate school is captured by Paul's words early in Ephesians: "It's in Christ that we find out who we are and what we are living for" (Ephesians 1:11 *The Message*). He says to the community in Asia Minor that in Jesus we discover three essential meanings: We learn *who* we are. We find *others* to help us read the story of our life. And we find out *why* we exist. We learn those facts as we take notice of the unfolding story of our lives together. All of Paul's writings are written to communities. North American individualism makes it hard for us to read biblical texts well; they are written to communities, churches, congregations, house churches and neighborhoods. They are about the work God is doing to make things right in the world, to bring together whole communities, and not only for personal gain and self-development. Mentoring is ultimately about something larger than one individual.

GROUNDED IN LIVED EXPERIENCE

Mentoring emerges from the Hebrew culture and way of knowing. It is rooted in what we might call *wisdom education* from the biblical literary form usually associated with Proverbs, Job, Ecclesiastes and some of the psalms. In the ancient biblical world, priests and prophets dealt primarily with religious life and morality while the sages offered guidance based on learning from life experiences. It is experiential knowledge that gives us practical, sometimes gritty insights on how to understand and live life. Wisdom writings are concrete and grounded in the stories of people in lived experience. They are grounded in the narrative of life. Wisdom, they seem to say, is only learned from encounters with the best and worst that life can bring; they are full of life and death, suffering and failure, awe and delight, epic moments and ordinary ones. Wisdom writings are like a handbook for how to make sense of what life has placed before you. And they share a belief that the source of wisdom is found in the Author, God, and not simply in one's self. Wisdom writings are insistent on this view of the universe: God is writing in the lives of people. People are cowriting story with God and family, households, coworkers, churches and neighborhoods.

"The fear of the LORD is the beginning of wisdom, and the knowledge of the Holy One is insight" (Proverbs 9:10). Bernard of Clairvaux got right to the heart when he said, "He who sets himself up as his own teacher becomes the pupil of a fool."[9] His conviction was pointed: we are formed spiritually in companionship with God *in the company of others*. Spiritual mentoring takes place as one helps another learn to read in co-creative *conspiracy* with the Holy Spirit. *Conspire* means "to breathe alongside" or in cooperation with another. The foundation is rock solid—Christian spiritual mentoring is directed and inspired by God's Holy Spirit.

Jesus took it a step further: "My Father is still working, and I also am working"—that's the foundational conviction (John 5:17) of mentoring as I have come to practice it. The living God is the source of the wisdom we seek; spirituality, therefore, is paying attention to the active presence of God.[10] God the Father is working, and Jesus, through the Holy Spirit, continues to work as well. Our job is to listen, ask questions, wonder out loud, muse and ponder and respond as we continue to puzzle about what we have seen and experienced. What Jesus began with his students qua friends, he continues with any who choose to be apprentices to the living rabbi in our midst. What Jesus began in the first century with the Twelve, breathtakingly, is not yet complete. In audacious faith we claim that his work continues in us, through us and with others as we learn, together, to pay attention.

Neuroscience is big business these days. Researchers are exploring our brains to help us understand how we think, learn and live. One conclusion is particularly apropos: our brains are taught to pay attention from an early age. "In the nursery we begin to learn what is important to pay attention to—and what isn't. It's also in the nursery that we learned that the world is far, far too vast to be mastered one bit at a time. We need to organize all the stuff of the world around us. We need priorities and categories that make navigating through life easier and more efficient."[11] Parents and other caregivers teach them how to sort, organize and prioritize. They are mirrors to infants in their development. They shape our biological processes through "mirror neurons," which "allow us to see what others see."[12] This happens in classrooms, sanctuaries, study halls, reading rooms—anywhere we practice the basic human skill of paying attention.

To what do we pay attention? William Barry's book title gives a clue: *Finding God in All Things*—no simple task.[13] We look and attend to the people, experiences, and events of the day and week. We look back to remember and relive. We look forward to anticipate, imagine, envision and hope. We look around to neighbor and stranger. We look inside to our own interior life. God's revelation is not limited to a certain time and place (worship), certain words (Scripture) or certain activities (religion), but has set an altar in the midst of all of life. We look at the spirituality of Jesus' own life as a first-century Jew. Grounded in daily life, we stop, look, listen, wait, question, discover and find God in all facets of life. What the centuries teach is to be unafraid of where, when and how to look for God. God's presence and voice are often nearby in the familiar and within, and he speaks in unexpectedly common ways.

- Whose voices have I heard in the past days?

- Which voices sounded louder, more insistent or stronger than others?

- Which ones whispered with a gentle word of welcome, invitation or encouragement?

- What sense of presence and voice came from unexpected places?

- What sense of presence and voice came from familiar and commonplace voices?

- What experiences left me most distracted, wounded or upset, and which experiences gave me hope, joy and delight?

- Where did I hear whispers of immortality or the still, small voice of God in recent days?

Always the spiritual exercises of reflection invite us to new vision for mission (what's next in my obedience to God?) and to old business (what needs to be finished, actualized and completed?). Feelings can include suffering or compassion (to feel with another). Compassion moves us outward toward others in solidary; suffering often moves us inward to our own, most immediate needs.

GOOD GROUND

I did some teaching in Alaska a few years ago. It was a privilege I won't forget. The Murdock Charitable Trust of Vancouver, Washington, created a leadership mentoring program titled Mentoring Matters. I was one of three lead teachers along with another half dozen senior mentors. One of our students who became a senior mentor was an Eskimo woman who works in pastoral ministry in a remote tribal community on the western edge of Alaska. I didn't know what to make of Dorothy when I first met her. She was quiet, a bit detached and possibly too shy to have much to say—at least, that's what I thought until she opened her mouth to speak for the first time. Whenever she spoke it seemed all of us knew she had wisdom in every word. In her tribal tongue, she showed me readily why she was chosen to be a leader in this group. She is a deeply spiritual woman, a wise woman, tested by hard life and experienced in hard ministry in the wilderness of Alaska so that her wisdom runs as deep as her spirituality. I quickly found myself humbled by the foolishness of my first impression. Later, she tried to teach me an Eskimo phrase (I'm sure I still can't pronounce it as she did); she said to me one day, "This is you: *noona lutkind*. Keith, this is who you are . . . who we all can be."The words *noona lutkind* mean "good ground." Good ground is receptive soil, ready for what will be planted. It is a statement of both how God sees our lives and how the work of mentoring proceeds. Jesus used the metaphor of soil and seed to teach his followers that sometimes we are good ground and sometimes hard, distracted or resistant ground. Mentoring proceeds as mentees pay attention to the plot unfolding in the soil of their life.

That too is where good mentoring of others begins. Dorothy's gentle words were spoken at a time in my own life when I didn't feel like particularly good ground but rather bad soil. I felt resistant to the Holy Spirit rather than receptive, but her words helped to soften my resistance as they declared an identity she saw in me— *good ground.* The Author who created humankind from the very ground itself used a wise Eskimo woman to help me read my story through her kindness.

In the sections between chapters, you will find brief reflections surrounding either a metaphor of mentoring or a useful resource or concept for mentoring. I hope these pictures and resources offer a more complete portrait of what we actually do in the work of mentoring.

Spiritual Mentoring
as Hospitality

How mentors approach the task of spiritual mentoring is mostly determined by their own understanding of spirituality itself. For some, spirituality is knowing certain things about God; mentoring therefore becomes focused on cognitive information. For some, spirituality is doing certain things for God; mentoring therefore becomes focused on particular spiritual disciplines. For me, spirituality is a living response to the living God who invites us into the friendship described by Jesus of his disciples; mentoring therefore is well described as hospitality.

Margaret Guenther speaks of hospitality as "welcoming the stranger" and describes in detail how she prepares the space for guests who arrive from somewhere on a journey to someplace else.[1] There's a simple elegance to her thoughtful preparation of the room with comfortable seating, flowers and a hearty welcome to the guest. She pays attention to the physical setting because she believes hospitality is spatial as well as spiritual. Henri Nouwen took it further when he said many years ago, "It is possible for men and women and obligatory for Christians to offer an open and hospitable place where strangers can cast off their strangeness and become our fellow human beings. . . . That is our vocation: to convert the hostis into a hospes, the enemy into a guest, and to create the free and fearless space where brotherhood and sisterhood can be formed and fully experienced."[2] If you dare, read the words again and remember a time and place someone has helped convert you into a guest.

What does a host provide for the guest?

- A place or setting prepared for the well-being and comfort of the guest. For the mentor, that means choosing a location that allows for privacy and confidentiality where prayer and story-telling can be comfortably enabled.

- An awareness that the guest is on a journey from another place and is not likely to settle down and remain permanently in the home of the host. The good host doesn't take over and tell the guest how to understand everything they have already experienced but welcomes them into their space and creates a place of comfortable conversation. Similarly, the mentee has a story from other places in his or her life and is journeying to a future in another place.

- Basic information needed for the time of the visit—for overnight guests, they show them where they will sleep, where the bathroom is, what they may eat and where to find beverages to drink. The mentor also guides a process to provide the mentee with enough familiarity to feel safe, secure and welcomed. For Margaret Guenther, that means she doesn't keep records of the "secrets" and stories told by the mentee but honors them in her memory.[3] "We must have a discerning eye, but we are not diagnosticians in a clinical sense, for we risk diminishing our guests if we reduce them to symptoms and measurements. The person sitting opposite me is always a mystery. When I label, I limit."[4]

St Benedict told his community: "Let all guests who arrive be received like Christ."[5] Through the centuries, spiritual mentors have been good hosts, opening their time, questions and ears to others just as they open their homes to welcomed guests.

God as Author

The words startled me. I suspect that was the anonymous writer's point in this revision of Psalm 23.

The Lord is *not* my shepherd
I am in want
Rest evades me
I cannot resist the tyranny of the urgent
My energy is sapped
I am without direction on some aimless path
Bringing nothing but dishonor to myself and those around me
Especially when I run through the dark valley of death
I am terror filled
For I am alone
Your absence leaves me barren and inconsolable
I am famished, and sounded by vultures
I am an unwelcome burr in your saddle
Dust kicked from a shoe
My cup is empty
Your love keeps missing me
Day after day
I will live alone, in an empty apartment forever.

The first time I read the words out loud, I was amused by the obvious reframing of Psalm 23, but now I feel the despair, loneliness and sadness in the heart of the one who penned the words. Where you start matters. You can start, as did the revisionist poet, without belief in a caring shepherd who walks with you. You can start, as do some, with a belief that we are alone in the universe. Spiritual mentoring instead starts with a conviction that God is Author, writing on the days and nights of our lives. Spiritual mentoring is a bold act of faith that God is active in the unfolding moments of our story.

I learned this best from Jayber Crow, the fictional barber in Wendell Berry's book of the same name. Jayber was orphaned twice as a child—first in the death of his birth parents and later in the passing of beloved Aunt Cordie and Uncle Othy who took him in to raise him as their own child. After some years away, he returned to the town he knew as home in the midst of a raging flood. He saw the drama of lives changed in minutes by torrential rains and uncontrolled river currents. He saw life altered as the floods carried straw, leaves, sticks, boards, barns and houses away. "The whole world, it seemed, was cast adrift, riding the currents, whirled about in eddies, the old life submerged and gone, the new not yet come."[1] But he saw more than destruction, trauma and change. I am captivated by the raw faith of his words: "And I knew that the Spirit that had gone forth to shape the world and make it live was still alive in it. I just had no doubt. I could see that I lived in the created world, and it was still being created. . . . The Spirit that made it was *in* it, shaping it and reshaping it, sometimes lying at rest, sometimes standing up and shaking itself like a muddy horse, and letting the pieces fly."[2] At another point he says, "This is one of the things I can tell you that I have learned: our life here is in some ways marginal to our own doings, and our doings are marginal to the greater forces that are always at work."[3]

GREATER FORCES ARE AT WORK

The "greater forces" are the movements of God's Spirit, the Author of our stories, in our lives. Spiritual mentoring is not the inventive, individual work of the mentor, pastor, teacher or friend who tries to make something happen in the life of another. It is, instead, the work of reading what the Author is already writing in the days and nights of the mentee. Different than other forms of mentoring, spiritual mentoring starts with faith in the presence and voice of the living God. This is faith-filled work in every sense: it starts with a belief that God's presence and voice may be known and heard, and it moves us to pay attention to presence and voice from week to week as we meet for mentoring. Learning to read life as story in this way starts with confident belief in an Author who is at work in writing this story. This conviction answers strategic and practical questions:

- Where does initiative come from for mentoring? God's Holy Spirit takes the lead on all spiritual growth; mentoring is responsive to the leading of the Spirit. That's why learning to read your life as story is so important.

- What is the work of mentoring? The ministry of spiritual mentoring is primarily a ministry of discernment, attention getting and attention giving, not of creating or forcing growth.

- What is the role of the mentor? The mentor is not a passive bystander but active in the deepest possible meaning of waiting and listening for presence and voice. Strategies for spiritual formation, however, may include assertive and forceful intervention in the life of the mentee by the mentor, but always with attention to the movement of God's Spirit. Learning to wait in the Spirit and listen for the Spirit is core curriculum for the mentor.

How can we develop the skill and instinct to read attuned to God as Author? Reading biblical narrative is one of the best ways I know because it offers a pathway and portrait of how the Spirit works. Jesus held nothing back when he talked about the one who would follow him—the Spirit of Christ. It was not rhetorical metaphor but announcement: "I will not leave you orphaned; I am coming to you. In a little while the world will no longer see me, but you will see me; because I live, you also will live. On that day you will know that I am in my Father, and you in me, and I in you" (John 14:18-20). This one, Jesus, who had walked in their world, was coming to them again—this time in the person of the Holy Spirit. Luke 1:35 and Acts 1:8 are both announcements about One who will come to come to bring purposeful power along with visible and audible outcomes. "A child will be born" was promised and it happened. "You will be baptized with the Holy Spirit" was promised and it happened. Power to speak gospel in other tongues was promised and it happened. The pathway of the Spirit is mysterious, unseen and not easily understood. But biblical narratives show us the outcomes. People were changed; they saw things, heard things and said things.

In addition, biblical narratives offer a corrective to a commonly held misunderstanding. Gospel insists on one primary thing: the text is about God. Most of us might think the text is about *me*—*my* deliverance, *my* salvation, *my* forgiveness and redemption. A friend lamented recently, "I just want to be happy." But the biblical narratives don't promise all things to bring me happiness. They are pictures of what God has done and glimpses of what God intends for the world. If you read the biblical text and always see yourself as the primary hero or action figure of the story, chances are you have missed the point. If you read biblical stories and find only victory, triumph and success for yourself, then again, you have missed the point. Instead of being a story about you, what if biblical texts are ways to help us see the intersections of our lives with the life-giving Spirit of the world? What if they are meant to change our imagination to see our lives as Spirit-alive, Spirit-saturated and Spirit-infused? Then they draw us to the humble practice of listening for God's still, small voice. If we view them that way, they become a portrait of how the Spirit works— unseen and mysterious, in gently whispered hints and nudges, and sometimes in the wind of great power. Most of my experience is the former—I feel gently called, encouraged or directed. God's voice in my life is not usually loud but more like a whisper; God's voice in Scripture, however, is often thunderous and hard to ignore. When I write those words I know they sound both naive and unformed to many readers. *I want clear direction and a roadmap*, you may be thinking. I say, let the voices of the centuries teach us to listen.

One of our best teachers is the apostle Paul. He too hoped to find for himself and for others what we all long for. "I pray that the God of our Lord Jesus Christ, the Father of glory, may give you a spirit of wisdom and revelation as you come to know him, so that, with the eyes of your heart enlightened, you may know what is the hope to which he has called you, what are the riches of his glorious inheritance among the saints" (Ephesians 1:17-18). He looked for it with his eyes of faith. I'm not saying he didn't see; I am saying he didn't see it every day as he longed for it. To see God in our lives or to hear the voice of God or to see the movement of God in our story is hard work. Barbara Brown Taylor gives me helpful direction:

No matter how hard we try in the church, we will always mess some things up. And no matter how badly we mess some things up in the church, other things will keep turning out right, because we are not, thank God, in charge. With the eyes of your heart enlightened, you can usually spot the one who is. Just search for any scrap of the church that is still standing—any place where God is still worshipped, any bunch of faces that are still turned toward the light—and you will see him there bending over them, his hand upraised in endless blessing. It is he who fills all in all, whose fullness have spilled over into us. It is Christ the Lord.[4]

That's why I am drawn to the focus of Paul's writing: Jesus, the teacher, who is the most visible portrait we have of how Spirit works. Jesus told stories that were memorable and sometimes unclear; he ate meals with people and talked about simple and ordinary things as he taught them to sense what has been provocatively called the "sacrament of the present moment."[5]

Jesus taught in at least two ways: by the content of his words and by the actions of his life—by what he said and what he did. In Western Christianity we focus on his teachings; in the Global South, they are most interested in what he did—miracles, healings, prayers, symbolic actions, liturgical acts and exorcism. In both ways of teaching, Jesus seeks us out and invites us to walk with him; his invitation "follow me" is to follow in the way he taught and the words he taught.

Spiritual mentoring starts with a trust that *something* else is at work, *someone* else is active, *something more* is going on in the world around us. Greater forces are always at work. Not always seen but just as present as the flow of oxygen in our lungs. That something can be called *the already active presence of God*.[6] It is the ferocious belief that we are not alone in the universe. Despite what some believe is persuasive evidence to the contrary, I choose to stand in the centuries-deep company of apprentices of Jesus, immersed in faith.

PRESENCE AND BLESSING

John the apostle, writing from his own place of battle—in exile on the island of Patmos—declared his confidence even in the face of contradictory evidence:

> See, the home of God is among mortals.
> He will dwell with them;
> they will be his peoples,
> and God himself will be with them;
> he will wipe every tear from their eyes.
> Death will be no more;
> mourning and crying and pain will be no more,
> for the first things have passed away. (Revelation 21:3-4)

This is not a theological preference but rather a conviction about the true nature of the universe. In the same way, spiritual mentoring is an act of conviction that there is presence and blessing animating our world. Christian spirituality has always been built on the understanding that we start with the I Am of God, not the "I am" of self; we start with the I Am of God's movement toward us, not the "I do" of the self and not merely the I-thou of human interaction. Spirituality is our response to God's movement, presence and voice in our lives. The starting place is not a casual coincidence; it is an assertion of a worldview: God is, God is alive, God continues to act and speak into our lives. There isn't much middle ground on this; either God is the Easter God and Jesus is alive, raised from the dead and present, or . . . you fill in the rest.

In his letter to his community, John the apostle did not start with his readers, their problems, or even with himself. He started with a declaration of conviction about Jesus, the Word:

The Word was first,
   the Word present to God,
      God present to the Word.
The Word was God,
      in readiness for God from day one.

Everything was created through him;
      nothing—not one thing!—
      came into being without him.
What came into existence was Life,
      and the Life was Light to live by.
The Life-Light blazed out of the darkness;
      the darkness couldn't put it out. (John 1:1-5 *The Message*)

The Word is square one, the starting place, commencement, the opening and the beginning. The God who calls himself Alpha and Omega, the beginning and the end, is first. Paul said of Jesus, "He is the image of the invisible God, the firstborn of all creation; for in him all things in heaven and on earth were created, things visible and invisible, whether thrones or dominions or rulers or powers—all things have been created through him and for him" (Colossians 1:15-16). The creator of all things is the Author writing in the DNA and story of our lives. The action in the moment of creation is stunning: Yahweh breathed life into a body, and humankind was born as spiritual beings. We were *given* life.

GIVEN WHAT MATTERS

You know a statement is good when it lasts for generations. In a sermon in the 1800s Charles Spurgeon said, "Be not proud of face, place, race or grace." I first heard it as a question asked by a pastor of a church on the south side of Chicago, not far from where I was born. "What do you have that matters that you weren't given? What do you have that is truly important that you created on your own?" We each have four things that matter that we had nothing to do with: race, face, place and grace. It is easy enough to recognize that we didn't chose our race. No one checked a box that indicated an ethnic or racial preference. You were given your ethnicity. It makes the sheer arrogance of racism even harder to comprehend As if you had something to do with the selection of your race. You did not. Face means your DNA, family of origin, birth story and circumstance. You had absolutely nothing to do with your genetic makeup, family or birth. It was given to you, wanted or not, from someone else. Place is the location of your life as you began, including country, local setting, economic circumstance and social location. I was born to first-generation American-born parents whose own parents immigrated to Chicago from Sweden around the turn of the twentieth century. One grandpa was a contractor, the other a builder. From that blue-collar origin, my life moved to suburban Chicago to an almost 100 percent white, middle- and upper-middle-class community. I had nothing to do with being born in the United States or in those circumstances. The most important is the last—grace. If you are a follower of Jesus you know you had nothing at all to do with the gift of grace; it was the gift of God the Father through Jesus Christ the Son in the work of the Holy Spirit.

Arguably, those are our four human essentials—race, face, place and grace—and we had nothing to do with them. That was the point of Spurgeon's famous nine-word sermon: we are where we are because of choices made since those beginnings, but we did not arrive on our own. This is an echoing theme in this book. We did not arrive at this moment in our lives alone. We are not meant to do the work of living life on our own. We are marked by the Author's active presence in our lives in face, place, race and grace. We reflect the image of the Author who writes our story within us as we live our life—*imago Dei*, the image of God. We reflect God's relational nature and character in the formation of our lives. The Author has written into our story qualities and character that influence how we live life. And living life is the point, after all.

Eugene Peterson is one of those I consider a mentor in my life, although we've had only occasional contact. He has done more to shape my thinking about God and spirituality than anyone I know. He said,

> The end of all Christian belief and obedience, witness and teaching, marriage and family, leisure and work life, preaching and pastoral work is the *living* of everything we know about God: life, life, and more life. If we don't know where we are going, any road will get us there. But if we have a destination—in this case a life lived to the glory of God—there is a well-marked way, the Jesus-revealed Way. Spiritual theology is the attention that we give to the details of living life in this way. It is a protest against theology depersonalized into information about God; it is a protest against theology functionalized into a program of strategic planning for God.[7]

Our stories are animated in the details and particularities of events in our life. The meaning of these details is only understood as we learn to read in faith. Making meaning of events is more than memory, but it requires the eyes of memory to see. I picture myself on the steps of our home as my father climbed the stairs to tell me that my grandmother had died. We met halfway up the stairs. Somehow I felt the trembling change in my world before I heard him speak the words. It is a vivid, almost palpable moment as I still can both feel and smell the starched white shirt of my business-executive father. I don't remember the words he spoke, but somehow the moment became etched in a terrific collision of grief and rare physical affection. I felt loss and I felt love. I see and feel the memory as acutely as if it were this morning. The details are the vocabulary of an unfolding plot; the meaning can come only as we read the unfolding story and see it as more than a collection of random events.

As Jayber Crow stands on a hillside looking at the eroded remains of his childhood home, the landscape punctuated with a single deteriorating chimney that once warmed the house and fed them all, he acknowledges, "Our history is always returning to a little patch of weeds and saplings with an old chimney sticking up by itself."[8] Each story holds its own little patch of weeds and saplings and chimney. My story holds the particularity of the memories and meaning my inner storyteller continues to tell. My story is a place to which I return to feel or resist feeling, to make sense or just to make meaning. My story is something I need to tell because it is mine to know and to give. Jayber came to believe that something more was going on than could be seen or heard. He believed that there are "greater forces that are always at work."[9]

TESTIMONY

I started my story of faith at a table with various authors, each in their own place of redemption, delight, desert, battle and exile, who sounded a clarion call: spirituality is lived in the presence of a living Abba, Father-God. It is not individual heroism in the face of threat or stoicism in the face of opposition; it is the witness of people with eyes to see and ears to hear. In the church days of my childhood, we would have called it *testimony*. To testify is to declare with conviction what one has seen, heard, felt and known. Wednesday-evening prayer meetings and some Sunday nights were given to a time long since lost in my church life—a time when people briefly stood to tell the story of what they had seen God do in their lives. The rest of us were simply there, seated, as if in an arena to witness. We listened and perhaps murmured a word of assent (we didn't speak very loud; after all, we were conservative Baptist folks in a white, suburban congregation), but mostly we were there to witness in our own way, to be present as another told his or her story, to listen and to come alongside. Part of the role of those listening to testimony is to give witness to it and to affirm the work of God in each person's life. I cannot escape the memories deeply etched in my soul: those finite, flawed and failed human beings—homemakers, teachers, custodians, business executives, blue-collar workers and shopkeepers—stood to give witness to what they had seen, heard, felt and knew that God was doing in their stories. Like John 1, it was an experience *in vivo*, a living story in time and space.

The heart of spiritual mentoring is not a schema or series of steps; it is a sensitive movement toward paying attention to God, to self and to the life of the mentee by both mentor and mentee. It is not a simple list of procedures but a dynamic and wise relationship that discerns next steps in the journey of faith; it creates what may be called a holding environment—a safe place in which to explore, question, struggle, probe, wonder, learn, unlearn and listen. Richard Rohr makes a clear-cut observation: "The only consistent pattern I can find is that all the books of the Bible seem to

agree that *somehow God is with us and we are not alone.*"[10] If you are
inclined to skim past those words, do not. This is the bedrock theological assumption of all spiritual mentoring: God is with us and
we are not alone. "One great idea of the biblical revelation is that
God is manifest in the ordinary, in the actual, in the now, in the
concrete incarnations of life. That's opposed to God holding out
for the pure, the spiritual, the right idea or the ideal anything."[11]

SEEN AND UNSEEN, THE PLOT UNFOLDS

In the midst of life's busyness, we are helped as people of faith to
remember one defining truth: the Lord *is* with us, seen or unseen,
felt or not. Recently, as I prepared for my workday, I saw clouds
from my office window looking out onto Elliot Bay on the waterfront of Seattle. It was early, shadowy, and the clouds seemed to
pivot from the waterfront up Wall Street past my window. There
was a foggy darkness in the air and then, just for the briefest of
moments, a sliver of sunlight splashed into my windows on the
fourth floor. From foggy darkness to bright lightness in an instant. It quickly passed from one end of Wall Street to the other.
It was a fleeting moment, a whisper of a promise—a gentle
moment that appeared and was gone like the kindest brush of
one hand on another.

But was it really gone? Or just out of our sight for the moment?
The sunlight passed, but I knew it was not truly gone. We live in
shadows and darkness, in moments like that and maybe longer
moments of night, but we live as a community of faith in the
presence, surrounded by, sheltered in, "under the canopy," as the
ancient Jews would have said. By faith we claim there is presence—
the living Lord lives—in moments when we see with confidence
and when we are filled with uncertainty. This again is where I
choose to begin. Our experience of God is like my experience of

light that morning—I saw it for an instant and then it was gone, or so it felt. Spirituality is learning to pay attention to the presence of God *in everything*. It is a bold claim that God's voice can be heard and God's presence known in all things. It is a bold claim that says we live our life in the blessing of the already active presence of God. It was there before we showed up. It is there when we do show up. We are not alone even in the moments of our deepest loneliness. We are not on stage singing solo even when it feels like the orchestra is out for lunch.

Writing from the research of neuroscience, Cathy Davidson says, "Whatever you see means there is something you do not see. And then you are startled or distracted, lost or simply out for an adventure, and you see something else. . . . From infancy on, we are learning what to pay attention to, what to value, what is important, what counts."[12] We can train our attention to things that seem to matter most to us. We can realize that retraining our focus is a means to new learning. I don't think she was talking about God in her conclusion, but her words apply to our attunement to the presence of God in our life: "The fact that we don't see it doesn't mean it's not there."[13] Attention giving is about focus, intention and collaboration. My board of trustees stood on the twenty-fourth floor of a building in downtown Seattle for our meeting. The rooftop gave us stunning views of the city in all directions. As I walked past two trustees excited about something north of the building I heard one of them say, "What am I looking at?" It is one of the essential questions of mentoring.

Reading your life as story starts, in a biblical sense, with an Author who cowrites your life with purpose, intention and direction. It is not prescripted in detail but cocreated, cowritten and lived in relationship. Spiritual mentoring is about attentive listening *to* God, not speaking *for* God as if the mentor knows the mind of God in all matters. The risk for spiritual mentors is that we sit in a position to assume or be told that we speak for God and may subtly begin to believe that we replace the voice of God with our own. That is reason enough to say no to the job! There is danger in being a mentor because you can come to believe you hold answers, truth, insight, wisdom and knowledge.

Spiritual mentoring is instead both more complex and simpler: it is listening together to the life of the mentee *in the presence of God*. "Spiritual direction [mentoring] takes place when two people agree to give their full attention to what God is doing in one (or both) of their lives and seek to respond in faith."[14] It is simple: we listen to the ordinary moments of life. It is complex: we listen to the ordinary moments of life. We are trained in our culture to pay attention to the momentous, glamorous and dramatic, but "the Scriptures and our best pastoral traditions train us in a different approach: notice the small, persevere in the commonplace, appreciate the obscure."[15]

Spiritual Mentoring
as Farming

I grew up on the south side of Chicago within miles of a defunct steel mill. We moved to the western suburbs where gardening meant flowers and mowing meant two hours to cut a large corner lot of lawn. I was not a farmer, but I had dirt under my fingernails; as I grew, I took every opportunity I could find to plant in the ground—flowers to see, yes, but vegetables to eat and fresh, seasonal food to love. I set out one year to transform a flowerless quarter acre of suburban Minnesota into a garden of shrubs, flowers, shade plants, onions, Swiss chard, tomatoes, squash and peppers. Each January I eagerly studied the catalogs and imagined the overflow of produce and the riot of colors to be shared with others. We imagined our yard as a kind of English garden out the back door of the house. It happened—but, to my surprise, it took twelve years. Annuals would bloom and grow and give an immediate explosion of color, but only for a season and then they were gone. Perennials were the best to plant but slowest to grow. The lilacs, sumac and apple tree—well, they weren't in a hurry at all. They flowered and produced fruit only in their own good time. I could not hurry them along. I had to wait until they were ready. When I owned five acres of partially wooded land in Island County, Washington, I planted Douglas fir trees only to find their growth glacially slow, much slower than my dream for another one-hundred-foot tree.

We returned to Minnesota some time ago to see what had become of a three-foot Colorado blue spruce we found on sale one October on a drive in the country. The scrubby little twisted and deformed tree I had planted in the ground was now thirty feet tall, brilliantly blue, and majestic in size, shape and scope. I can say with pride that it is stunning, but it took almost fifteen years to grow. Mentoring as farming is one of the most important images I can suggest. The implications for spiritual formation aren't hard to see:

- Patience is in order. You will learn to pass on the quick fix or the sudden conversion in favor of slow, perhaps steady growth. The work is slow, tedious at times and seemingly without results. The growth is hard to measure from week to week; it is better to look at the long view instead of the short, to look back over months instead of week by week.

- Suddenly, it seems, there is growth and produce and beauty, but it happens thanks to careful attention to the details of planting seeds, cultivating, weeding, watering and waiting.

- There is both science and art in farming, gardening and mentoring. There is always a time to plant and cultivate what has begun to come to life before you, just as there is always something new (or old) to study and learn. You study the texts of agronomy and Scripture; you spend time in the presence of artists who can teach you skillfully and with grace. You become an apprentice to the centuries. You delight in the discipline of the science and the joy of the art.

Life as Text

Paula D'Arcy said with wonderfully evocative clarity, "God comes to us disguised as our life."[1] Perhaps that's why we need mentors most of all—to help us see what is hidden or misdirected, camouflaged or only suggested. God isn't shy but chooses, some of the time, to come to our lives as Jesus came to our world—in a form that didn't simply broadcast divinity. Why is that? Is it a test or a trick or simply a foil to see if we care? I don't think so. Jesus embodied divinity in the body of a particular little Jewish boy born on the edges of power, wealth and significance. Bethlehem was a small, unimportant town, a bit off the beaten path—not DC, London, New York or Beijing. He walked among us, lived among us, learned among us and taught us to take notice as we live our actual life. In academic language we speak of particularity—that story is grounded in time and place, specific and real people, events, and circumstances.

The great classical spiritual teachers of our history all seemed to know this. Thomas á Kempis wrote *The Imitation of Christ* as a kind of handbook for ordinary people to grow in prayer, meditation and piety. St. Francis de Sales said, "My purpose is to instruct those who live in town, within families, or at court, and by their state of life are obliged to live an ordinary life."[2] John Wesley's teaching included books on spirituality written specifically for families and children. Benedict of Nursia understood the meaning of work, especially physical labor, as essential to spiritual growth and ordered his monastic community around practices that included prayer for the tools with which they did their daily chores. And profoundly, Benedict taught his monks to listen reverently with the ear of the heart.

IN THE DETAILS

We learn to read the story of our cultural time and place only if we have learned to read the particularity of our own story. J. B. Philips once contrasted the humble circumstances of Jesus' birth with another option he imagined God had. God might have chosen to hang woofers and tweeters in the heavens to declare the message *about* Jesus, but he chose instead the pathway of incarnation, which is the pathway of particularity. He called earth "the Visited Planet."[3] Rather than broadcast information and good news, God chose to penetrate the earthly planet with one who lived his story in the presence of first-century people in Galilee—in a particular time, in a particular place. No wonder people have struggled to understand incarnation. God's universal self compressed and transformed into the body, mind, spirit and culture of a particular Jewish boy in the first century. A planet visited by the Creator of the universe? It's the dramatic revelation that Christian faith is grounded in lived events, historical moments in time and space—in Jesus' birth, through his life in Galilee, through his death by Roman executioners and beyond. Jesus made breakfast on the beach for his friends after the historical event we call Easter—the resurrection. Whether this is event and not merely metaphor matters. It matters because it is a tangible revelation that God once intruded in history in the person of Jesus and a declaration that God continues to walk in presence among us through the person of the Holy Spirit. The world is alive with voice and presence; there is an Author whose pen is at work every day in the cocreation of your story. If not, then we are alone in the world, dependent on human ingenuity, insights and information. The incarnation is the best way to know who God is.

Spiritual mentoring is learning to read the unfolding particularity of your life with the help of another reader, someone we call a mentor. The word *mentor* was first used by Homer in *The Odyssey*.[4] In Greek mythology Mentor was left in charge of a young man, Telemachus, as Odysseus left to fight in the Trojan War. His task was to teach a curriculum that was broad and deep: soul, spirit and mind were the recipients of his work, which means there was information, to be sure, but more, there was formation, wisdom and transformation. He did not share the banking metaphor of education in which we deposit knowledge into the brain in the form of cognitive data; Mentor helped give shape and form to the heart and soul of young Telemachus. It was formational teaching through experience and story. Disseminating information is not storytelling; it is not formational. Mentor, we could readily say, helped Telemachus read his life as story. He opened his imagination to know the universe itself is a story to be read, as are families, organizations, churches and businesses. Some things can never be learned by reading a book. Spirituality is incomplete as text only. Learning to read transforms the world from disparate, random events into a sacred story. Mentoring, I say, is the careful, respectful and engaged reading of another.

The root word for *Bible* originally just meant "books," a collection of certain types of writing—law, poetry, prophetic writings, instructions for holy living, sermons, admonitions and letters. But for those with ears to hear it has become a story with narrative progression and development. It is read for meaning that is crafted most often in narrative form. We know commandments and Deuteronomic laws because they are intertwined with stories of people with names like Moses, Aaron and Miriam. We know the poetry of psalms and wisdom writings because we've read the narration of David's story, just as we know wisdom proverbs because they are told in stories of Solomon and Job. Prophetic fury is proclaimed in stories of Isaiah, Jeremiah, Amos, Hosea, Joel and Malachi. Synagogue spirituality is the story of the return of an entire people from decades in exile in the stories of Nehemiah, the urban planner, and Ezra, the one who read Torah for all to hear. We know Jesus' teachings because we have been told the story of his life, death and resurrection in relationship with people like Mary, Peter, James, John and, of course, Judas. We know Paul's theology because we learn his story of conversion, apostleship, church planting and suffering. Names matter because they are a sign of relationship; I don't *know* you unless I can call you by name. In a crowded train station or airport, the rushing sounds of travelers can cease when I hear my named called out loud. Names are markers of our story. We are people with names whose lives are stories to be read

Other people help us notice the text of our life, mining for wisdom in the unfolding plot of our story in the presence of God's Spirit. Wendy, my wife, and I sat at our favorite breakfast place on Puget Sound with a view of Mount Rainier, the Cascade Mountains and the distant skyline of Seattle. Over coffee, eggs and pancakes, we did what we always do—talked about our lives and allowed what topics would arise to arise. Over many years we have learned how to do that well—no agenda, no topic, but a gentle space that allows good conversation to develop. "Who was the most influential person in your life?" she asked. She was thinking about her life in terms of generations past with a remaining aging parent and future generations with our own seven grandchildren scattered across the country. I needed time to think about my answer. Finally, a list emerged, an ensemble of names of people whose influence had shaped my pastoral ministry and my work in higher education, leadership, spirituality and theology. Some were professors or colleagues, some were writers whose work had shaped my own. Some are living and close, some are gone, but together they form an orchestra of artists who shaped me, changed my life, guided me, critiqued me, affirmed me, loved me and motivated me for the work of my life.

The question came from Wendy's heart, not from my own conscious thought that morning. It was prompted by a life shared in which space is created for planned and spontaneous musing about life and always for great questions—questions that require thought and may not be answered quickly or easily. It was prompted by my best soul friend who has always asked the questions that I most need to ask but may most prefer to avoid if left to my own devices. And it punctuates what we know instinctively at a deep level: we need others to come alongside us with questions, curiosity and presence.

I heard once that the design of graduation robes is so big because they need to provide space for such an orchestra of artists who helped bring us to that moment of commencement. We do not come to the present moment on our own. We are none of us independent contractors in life who have arrived wherever we are on our own. It is a symphonic work, not a solo. Our voice may be the loudest or most dominant at one time or another; we may be on center stage at a given moment, but the story of our life is not about the heroic individual. We are shaped by others whose influence, whether acknowledged or not, has shaped us. Those people are mentors in their own right—parents, siblings, spouses, children, loved ones and friends who have their own way to probe and prompt us to go further to read our story.

The end game in spiritual mentoring is to sit with another person in the "amazing inner sanctuary of the soul"[5] to listen to the speaking voice of the living God in that time and place in the mentee's life. Unless those words describe reality—an authentic place to which we can go—mentoring is just two people hanging out together sharing ideas. There's nothing wrong with that, but mentoring is more. We are not simply two people helping each other with our own ideas, insights and thoughts; we are able to sit together in the presence of the living God in that sanctuary of the soul. Not two, but three. That makes all the difference, for we are there to listen to more than the speaking of human voice; we are there in bold faith listening for God's whisper, nudge, echo or thunder. But it rarely comes in a loudspeaker, crash of thunder or whirling wind. It most often comes slowly, over time, as we sit in conversation about ordinary things *that matter*. We know they matter because they puzzle us or are recurring themes or are simply curious. My best mentors have known that. They didn't force conversations about "spiritual" things as much as "life" things. They didn't manipulate conversations about the latest book they had read about spiritual theology as much as asked questions about the latest meanderings of my spirit. Often their questions weren't profound except they echoed in a deep place in me. They never seemed in a hurry. They always seemed comfortable with silence. And, over time, we knew we had spent time in the presence of blessing and voice.

HOW TO READ STORY

Story is a large word that can include fairy tale, comedy, tragedy, biography, world history, biblical narrative and entire libraries of literary and life content. There is not a single method for reading story. Elsewhere I have suggested a series of reading methods that enhance our skills for reading multiple texts. Use the following list to suggest various ways to reflect and "read" the unfolding story of your life. The mentee needs to become self-aware by reading his or her own story with the help of the mentor. The mentor needs to practice the skill of reading story in many forms.

1. Read like a reporter, looking for descriptions of "facts" (what is heard, seen, tasted, touched and smelled). Look first at the details of what is told.

2. Read like an artist, looking at the imagery in words chosen to describe events and figures of speech, especially similes and metaphors, to describe what the events felt like to the writer. Look for hints or whispers of God's voice in your life today.

3. Read like an exegete, trying out different interpretations as you speculate about possible meanings. What might this event mean for the larger plot? Is this a defining moment? Look for the beginning of meanings in recent events in your life.

4. Read like a geographer for location and point of view. Where you stand changes what you see. What biases, blind spots or worldviews are at work in the story? Look to see how your perspective affects how you feel about events in your life.

5. Read like an English teacher to study syntax, patterns of grammar and the formation of words. What patterns are repeated? What changes in the tone of the book? Who is speaking? When? Why? What words seem important? Are there words that trigger emotions of anger, sadness, shame, joy or longing? Look especially to see whose voice is loud in the narrative right now.

6. Read like a classmate in a learning community where others will join you in asking great questions about what is being

written. What do the questions of others provoke for your own meaning making? What do they see in your story that you cannot see without the vision of others? Listen to what others are telling you, especially if their perspective gives a very different meaning than your own.

7. Read like a writer, looking for humor, irony, the juxtaposition of themes, tragedy, comedy and myth. Are there themes that repeat themselves that seem important?

8. Read like a librarian, looking for information, formation, transformation, literature, comedy, tragedy, history and science. Look for all that makes life fascinating.

9. Read like a reader: just keep on reading. Before you settle on a meaning, read it again. Read to savor the moments. What is especially enchanting in your story at present?[6]

REALITY CHECK

The canvas on which I'm painting images of mentoring can seem filled with warm colors that promise something sentimental. Two people engaged in spiritual conversations in the presence of God. The time is ready for revelation, epiphany, presence and the unleashing of the Holy Spirit in power, right? There may be candles, comfortable chairs, good coffee or tea—ambience all around. Reality check. Because God is the author, there is not much that is predictable when mentor and mentee meet. I will tell you the truth: Jesus comes and goes as he chooses. God doesn't show up on schedule in mentoring any more than in worship or prayer. There is nothing formulaic about this work. *We* show up; sometimes we ask, "What are we waiting for?" Sometimes we have an epiphany, and sometimes we are like the disciples at the ascension, standing and looking into the heavens, waiting, but we are not inactive. It is not a transaction for guaranteed results, as if we show up and God speaks on demand. It may work for movies on my TV, but not with God. But we are being changed as we read the details of our story.

I was in Missouri with my friend Jack. He said, "I've lived my entire life in Missouri but realized recently I don't know that much about the president that came from my state, Harry Truman, so I read a biography of his life." Jack often points me to good reading so I ordered the book online. I didn't check first, so I didn't know until I opened it on my iPad what I had signed up for: thousands of pages—not hundreds, but thousands. Thankfully, it was well written, and I enjoyed the voice of the writer and the subject. In mentoring, we read details. It is slow work because we are reading biography, not a Hollywood epic movie. Later, I suppose, we can read the CliffsNotes version or the highlights, but for now, we read details. We don't have a summary of the plot because the plot is still being written—by God, by us, with the reading teacher who is our mentor. We don't have a synopsis of the film version because the screenwriter hasn't released it yet. That might come later. For now, we live in the details.

So we show up and read what is being written in the ordinary movement of days and weeks. Impatient as small children, we may demand God's presence and full attention only to find ourselves in moments of listening, waiting and learning to read. The questions we ask as the novel unfolds are not all the same as reading the detailed biography as it unfolds, but the details will tell the story of the life that is being written before our very eyes. Does that sound like a betrayal of all that I've said about God as Author? Does it lower your expectations as mentor and mentee? I hope instead that it creates something authentic—patience for detail; enjoyment of the commonplace; respect for what is, in fact, being written by the Author; gratitude for time well spent in spiritual companionship; leisurely unfolding conversation and appreciation for questions that start the cycle all over again. We learn to decipher the ink strokes of the Author's pen as we read slowly, patient for detail through all of the events of life.

Spiritual teacher Carolyn Gratton wrote, "It is true that human beings do some of their navigating by their 'stars'— but human beings figure out somewhat more of their true direction, not by the high stars, but by stubbing their toes on things stuck in the mud they are slogging through."[7] I don't know anyone who can't identify with stubbed toes or getting stuck in the mud. It doesn't take long to create a list of some of those places where we get stuck:

- When our past life patterns break up. "Unasked-for changes comes in all sizes. It can be massive and catastrophic. . . . Unsought change also comes in personal and small-group sizes."[8]

- In early life transitions—education, marriage, new jobs, the birth of children, a move to a new city.

- In later life transitions—midlife, retirement and the end of life.

- In life-altering experiences of illness, chronic pain, and unexpected losses of job, relationship, health or friendship.

- When we face the limitations of our humanity through moral failure, physical boundaries of illness and age, emotional or psychological trauma, divorce, and catastrophic life events.

- When we are called on to care for others in the birth of children, for family in health crises or for aging parents.

- When we are confronted by the unexpected failure of others within our circles of relationship or household.

- When there is harm, trauma or abuse.

- When there is nothing at all—no change or momentum in life and ennui sets in.

- When life decisions need to be made that necessitate change of location, relationship, job or career.

Because life keeps happening, spiritual mentoring is never "one and done." Because life keeps happening, mentees learn to pay attention to the transitional moments of epic change *and* the seemingly obscure moments of routine and the quiet passing of time. That's life as it gets lived.

Core Curriculum

In the academic world in which I live, we use words like "core curriculum" to describe the missional convictions at the center of our education. It's hard work to describe the irreducible essence of our programs. Whenever I can, I ask other mentors or spiritual directors to tell me what they see as the outcome or the purpose of their conversations with a mentee. Most spiritual mentors, directors, companions, guides and friends agree on at least five essentials as necessary to spiritual formation. It may be inflated to call it the core curriculum, but I like the odds they got it right. This is what I have learned.

1. We do not come to spiritual maturity alone; we need the help of others who will come alongside us to help us make sense out of our spiritual lives. It is something built into our humanity and our history in the human family: spiritual formation is not a work done in the isolation of monastic cells or anchor holds, but in the community of everyday spiritual companionship. We need others who will keep us honest, love us, speak truth to us and walk the journey with us.

2. The content of spirituality is life, ordinary life, daily life, and the common things we do. "Simply put, spiritual direction is helping

people tell their sacred stories every day."[1] Maybe that's why it seems so hard—we get used to the rhythms of our common life and need fresh eyes to see what is there and fresh ears to listen with us for the voices that are all around.

3. God is present to us in ways that we can know, discern, hear or see as we practice paying attention. All of classical spirituality teaches us to pay attention—sometimes the preferred sense is hearing, sometimes it is seeing, touching or tasting. The body is involved in our spiritual work. "Spiritual direction is the contemplative practice of helping another person or group to awaken to the mystery called God in all of life, and to respond to that discovery in a growing relationship of freedom and commitment."[2]

4. The process of spiritual formation involves us in conversations, holy listening, wholly listening, deep listening, contemplative reflection and prayerful discernment. "Spiritual direction is a time-honored term for a conversation, ordinarily between two persons, in which one person consults another, more spiritually experienced person about the ways in which God may be touching her or his life, directly or indirectly. In our postmodern age, many people dislike the term 'spiritual direction' because it sounds like one person giving directions, or orders, to another. They prefer 'spiritual companionship,' 'tending the holy,' or some other nomenclature. What we call it doesn't make any real difference. The reality remains conversations about life in the light of faith. There was much to talk about, to sort out in the light of faith in those days when confusion in the Church became a daily reality."[3]

5. The work is slow and the results may be unspectacular, but it all matters. We will see the work and the results over time.

Spiritual practices lead to engagement with the heartbreak of the world on behalf of the poor, exploited, and those who are victims of prejudice or violence. Spiritual growth leads to caring for others, not merely self-interest. The journey inward toward spiritual maturity leads to a journey outward on behalf of others.

The Mentor as Coreader

Henry Owassa Tanner was one of the earliest African American painters and one of the most brilliant artists of his age. He was a student of the American artist Thomas Eakins, but as a good student he soon found his own art, style and technique. Many of his works in his maturity are works of spiritual content, like *The Resurrection of Lazarus*, but my favorite is one he painted in 1893. *The Banjo Lesson* shows a man, probably a grandfather, with a young boy sitting on his lap as he learns to play the banjo. The "teacher" holds the banjo while the young "student" strums the strings and tries to do the finger work of finding notes and chords. The setting is possibly a kitchen in a small house that speaks of comfortable familiarity. It is an intimate scene, most likely a family moment, but it suggests to me the interactive role of a mentor and mentee. The mentor can play the banjo—he or she knows something about the music and has developed the practices necessary to make the music. The mentee is there to learn from someone who has skill, insight and experience, which they need. But the mentor doesn't take over the lesson by playing *for* his young student; instead, as this painting shows, he creates a way for the child to become the learner. The grandfather doesn't sit *across* from the child, apart from him and distant as he shows him how well he can play; instead he joins with the boy to create a place for him to try his own hand at learning the music.

The intimacy of the grandfather and grandson is suggestive of the vulnerable relationship that mentoring creates. It is also suggestive of the relationship we have in the writing of our lives. There is an Author, I have said. God is writing our story in face, place, race and grace. God has started the story by imprinting us with *imago Dei*, the image of God, which becomes one shaping force in our lives as we reflect what God has already written into our DNA and nature. And, like the grandfather, the young boy is in on the process as he struggles to play his own music. He is the coauthor of the musical story he tells as he is held in holy and faithful love by the grandfather, just as we are coauthor in both writing and reading the soul work of our lives.

COMPANIONS BECOME COREADERS

Many cultures, including our own until not that long ago, have a valued practice of apprenticeship and rites of initiation. Boys become men only after a process of learning from the elders. Sometimes they are sent out on a quest to discern spiritual presence, but always in connection with the men of the village. Fathers taught their sons how to work in the fields, in the shop or factory, or in the vocation of the father. Women were mentored in the ways of womanhood and possibly motherhood by apprenticeship with the older women of the town, tribe or community. Girls learned the economics of managing homes, shops, families and commerce. Much of that has been lost in our more nomadic and individualistic culture. We have especially lost the rituals of transition other cultures have—for example, from boyhood to manhood in the bar mitzvah of Judaism or from girlhood to womanhood in the bat mitzvah. Or the sacred rituals of Native Americans or even the place of our own family traditions—getting a driver's license, starting the first job, going off to college, getting married or having children. My friend Chris Bruno has written a book on male apprenticeship with the provocative title *Man Maker Project: Boys Are Born, Men Are Made.* He writes to fathers about the mutuality of the relationship between fathers and sons on this journey together as he says, "You will find a major focus of this process also involves *your* heart and *your* story. . . . Your son was born into an already-occurring story—yours—and for him to know himself he will need you to know yourself."[1] Without that work, we can settle for lesser stories and miss the epic of God's story being written in us. "The world offers our sons nothing but small stories. If we want a generation of men to show up and change the world, to bring life and healing and restoration, then we must intentionally connect them to the greater narrative of God's kingdom. If we lose on this front, we lost altogether."[2]

Mentoring is as important today for spiritual growth as initiation and apprenticeship were for vocational formation in generations past. "I want to be present to people for spiritual growth, but it seems the only category people understand is that of a life coach. I am not a life coach," a young colleague said to me recently as we discussed the urgent need for spiritual mentoring as a recognized ministry for "the priesthood of believers." Spiritual mentoring is one of our most pressing ways to help others read the epic story of God in their own story.

Spiritual mentoring is one way we grow deep in knowing the living Lord in companionship. It requires the listening ears of another. It is essential apprenticeship. We do not find intimacy with God through intellectual exercises alone. We do not learn spirituality as a solo practice apart from others. We cannot do soul work well if we are always moving at high speed. *Information* is not formation. Instead of seeking more information, we should instead be asking, how does *formation* take place? At the insistence of a Christian teacher when I was in college I completed a series of fill-in-the-blank booklets called *10 Steps to Christian Maturity*. I think I answered the questions correctly. I adequately filled in every blank. I gained information. I completed all ten steps but at the conclusion of this exercise I was not mature—I was not even close. What programs for spiritual formation tend to ignore is our basic need for someone to come alongside and help us to embody the ideas. Spiritual mentoring is centuries deep. It started in homes, synagogues, fields, marketplaces, and jobs. It was not coincidental that Jesus created a community of learners and sent out ministry teams in twos and threes. Formation requires embodied relationship.

In the preface to his book on spirituality, *Reaching Out*, Henri Nouwen offers a portal into the most intimate inner space we possess: the spiritual center.

> The question about the spiritual life is a very challenging question. It touches the core of life. It forces you to take nothing for granted—neither good nor evil, neither life nor death, neither human beings nor God. That is why this question, while intimately my own, is also the question that asks for so much guidance. That is why the decisions that are most personal ask for greatest support. . . . I wanted to write this book because it is my growing conviction that my life belongs to others just as much as it belongs to me and that what is experienced as most unique often proves to be most solidly embedded in the common condition of being human.[3]

The same can be said of all forms of spiritual friendship—we learn in order to share with others; our story is written to be read again; "my life belongs to others just as much as it belongs to me."[4]

Embodied Presence: Crossing the Divine-Human Border

The island of Iona is a holy place. West of the mainland of Scotland, Iona has long been considered in Celtic spirituality one of the "thin places," a liminal place. It is "thin," they say, because the membrane between heaven and earth is a porous or permeable space; it creates a border between God and humankind. I heard such things with the ears of a skeptic until I departed the ferry from Fionnphort and walked about fifty feet onto the island. I couldn't put words to it then and can't explain it yet, but there was a sense of holiness unlike most places I have walked. I felt presence everywhere I wandered on the island. Because it is under Scottish land laws, one can walk the entire island including the private property of shepherds and farmers. I took off one day for a long, private quest for the quarry where I hoped to gather the green marble found only on the island. I never did find the quarry, but I found the morning remains of sheep droppings and mud into which I sunk deep above my shoes. When I departed Iona, I left behind that pair of jeans because I had no access to a washing machine and no one would travel with me back to the mainland smelling of the sheep.

Heaven and earth collide on Iona. I found myself surprised at first but later more comfortable with the sense of holy presence. I ran into a friend whom I had last seen on Whidbey Island in Washington State. I had said to her, "Let's meet again on the island," but had no idea it would be on another island, this one in Scotland. When we pray, the borders of heaven and earth overlap. The same is true in mentoring. Without the never-to-be-repeated incarnation of God in the body of Jesus of Nazareth, we would never know God, we would only know *about* God. The embodied presence of Jesus introduces us to relationship with the living God. Similarly, the embodied presence of a spiritual mentor helps us read the consecrated purposes of the living God as we cross the divine-human divide.

Heaven and earth also collide in Pike Place Market, on King County Transit, the Washington State Ferry, and on I-5 in Seattle. God inhabits our lives and our world. God initiates and is Author. But that is not all; stunningly, we are in on it, formally or informally, certified or not, clergy or lay. We all already practice spiritual friendship with others. We know something about it. We know something about the development of meaning, plot, characters and the progression of story, but I am convinced we need the help of spiritual mentors to see it more clearly, to ponder it and muse over what it all means. What God set loose in the incarnation of Jesus is, in fact, the way of spirituality. Heaven and earth collide. Daily experience intersects with consecrated purpose. Recruitment becomes calling. And—the part that some find hardest to accept— the voice of God will often take on the accent, timbre and words of presence embodied in a mentor who comes alongside as co-reader in the life of the mentee. It isn't simply randomness but divine intentionality. In every life, God shows up in the embodied presence of others we call the body of Christ. Spiritual friends are needed; spiritual mentors move the process deeper in intentionality and refined practice.

No Special Equipment Required

If I were to ask you to walk around your kitchen table, most readers could do that without thinking. Some, however, may have physical ailments or limitations that would make it more challenging. If I were then to ask you to tell me precisely what your body did as you walked around the table, it might take a while to sort it out. I recently had a knee replacement. It might sound a bit odd but the night before the surgery I became quite sentimental. In my own quirky way I said goodbye to a set of bones that had been given to me over sixty years ago. I traded them in for a new set of titanium and plastic. The surgery went well and then the real work began: learning to walk all over again. Within hours of the surgery, they had me up on my feet and were walking alongside me to keep me from falling. Think about it. I have walked for decades. I know intuitively how to take a step, but now it required concentration. I had to ask myself a new set of questions: What are your muscles doing? Which muscles are involved? What is the work of your lungs? What brain work is happening? How do quads, calf muscles and hamstrings interact in the simple process of taking steps? Walking is also called ambulation or locomotion. In scientific terms it is an inverted pendulum gait in which the body vaults over the stiff limb with each step. Even though you know how to walk, I wonder if you could have told me about your gait. Though you know how to walk, you are less skilled at *talking* about the technical steps (pun intended) and less certain about the details of its physiological dynamics.

Even so, we all know mentoring. We already know how to mentor because we have someone or several people in our lives whom we mentor or to whom we are a kind of apprentice. You probably already have in hand all the skills you need and all the equipment that is required: eyes to see, ears to hear, a heart to care, a story to tell, curiosity to wonder, willingness to engage another, love for another. It is the practice of spiritual companionship. Spiritual mentoring doesn't require special equipment, esoteric knowledge or skills available only to a very few. Whatever else you hear me say, hear this: you need to learn how to do the work of deep listening. Because we aren't that good at deep listening, most of us.

You most likely already know how to hike, but you need to prepare to climb a mountain. When I climbed Mount Rainier years ago, I spent months in preparation and training. I didn't think about *how* to walk as much as set out to build resilience for the rigor of a hike to the tallest mountain in the Pacific Northwest. Most of it was recognizing what I already knew how to do and learning to apply it in another context: walk, breathe, pace my energy, utilize my strength, rest in my weakness, walk roped up with two others. Yes, I needed to learn how to use the ice axe, but that is used primarily when someone falls down. Mostly I conditioned myself for the rigor of the climb. I walked up trails around the mountain, up and down a ravine just off 29th Street, and up and down Mount Si in North Bend. I spent time at St. Joseph hospital running steps in the back hallway to increase my lung capacity until a doctor caught me and warned me not to return. I walked because I needed to strengthen myself for the hardest climb of my life. The intensity of climbing a 14,411-foot mountain with a team of people required me to take what I already knew and learn it all over again in a new context.

THE LANGUAGE OF RELATIONSHIP

We are created as storytellers; it is our nature as humans. Story is the language of relationship. Formed in communities, humans have always found ways to gather around a common fire to tell stories of conquests and battles, victories and defeats, epic journeys and tragic adventures, and to teach the next generation about life in the family and community. All cultures have gathered for stories in the agora or commons, on stoops or in backyards, at tables in churches, synagogues, homes and city parks, with immediate and extended family, friends and neighbors. We are shaped by the stories we tell in family and community. Mine was a family story marked by the courageous choice of four young people, my grandparents, who left behind "the old country" in Småland, Sweden, to emigrate to

America seeking prosperity, fortune and hope for a future that seemed impossible to find in their economically distressed homeland. It was a story of faith spoken in bilingual congregations on the south side of Chicago that eventually scattered to suburbs west, south and north of the city. Those details matter in the shaping of identity for us all. "Remember where you came from" was a message I received, both spoken and unspoken. As my parents became more economically and financially successful, we knew to honor and value the blue-collar roots of our family— carpenters, builders, maids, house painters, grocers and farmers. My story is truncated and small if it is only the story of a Chicago-born white kid, raised in the suburbs, who goes on to teach and pastor. More fully, it is the story of people from Sweden named Anderson, Carlson and Liljedahl, whose great grandchildren are writing their stories in Massachusetts, Oregon, Washington and Ohio more than a century later.

During the Cold War, religious life was curtailed and, in some cases, banned altogether, as in the USSR. But as the light dawned in 1991 on a changed political reality, one thing became clear: religion was not dead. Christian faith had not been obliterated because it had been banned. Biblical teaching had not been silenced because it had been muted. While Bibles were made illegal, some courageous souls, often the *babushkas*, the older women, hid them—sometimes under floorboards or behind pictures on the wall, sometimes in their memory. But the remarkable story of the faith that persisted is that common, ordinary, sometimes uneducated people of faith became readers together of God's Word and of God in a hostile environment. Though religion was contested, companions who were sometimes singled out and persecuted for their beliefs found each other and *read* together. With candlelight around kitchen tables or in the hay-lofts of barns, they continued to read together. They read the narratives of the Old and New Testaments. And they talked of faith and life and continued to read life together. Some undoubtedly mentored others in the fierce faith they themselves practiced. They read not only words, stories and texts; they read their life in Moscow, Kiev and Chechnya with a desire to find the heart, mind and hope of God. They would tell you they lived as pilgrims learning to see with eyes of faith and to hear with ears of obedient trust.

My colleague Dan Allender goes even further as he declares, "You are a story. You are not merely the possessor and teller of a number of stories; you are a well-written intentional story that is authored by the greatest Writer of all time, and even before time and after time."[5] We live in the story that is our house; we live in the stories we tell and believe to be true. Our lives are not merely chronology, timelines or randomly unfolding and unrelated events; they are narrative. We are story. And, in the end, we need others to help us understand and complete the story in which we live. Allender approaches story with more honesty than I learned to. "Good stories tell about the intersection of desire ('subjective expectation') and tragedy ('cruel reality'). A story begins when our desires collide head-on with reality. Sometimes reality is impersonal, like a storm that sets into motion a flash flood that kills nine kids on a bus going to Bible camp. But other times the cruelty is volitional."[6]

Spiritual mentoring, in my view, belongs to the whole priesthood of believers. It is a normative thing we do for each other. I know there are some people with a special gift for mentoring. I have been the recipient of such a gift. One of my past mentors has a capacity for listening deeply and asking robust questions that has been unmatched in my life. He left me encouraged, bewildered, confident, disillusioned, certain, unclear and almost everything except ambivalent. He cared fiercely for me, I believe, and hoped imaginatively for my growth. He believed in me and saw things I would not recognize until years after we finished our work; he had a gift.

Others have given me another gift: they showed up in my life when I needed them. They too have been spiritual mentors. And they are as different as day and night. I suppose my belief that the work at hand belongs to the whole priesthood of believers means I am willing to leave it in the hands of amateurs, which I am. I value training, discipline and preparation for this work, but I am satisfied to leave it in the hands and hearts of amateurs. It is about reading, after all—something available to almost everyone. I suppose there are some professional readers, but most of us who read are not professionals but amateurs who bring the most important things we have to the table: our humanity, spirituality, curiosity, tentative humility and art. We are not experts, scientists, nor technicians in spirituality—and that's a good thing because it keeps us from becoming overly certain that we speak for God. As a "professional" churchman—exegete, theologian, pastor and preacher—I puzzled over texts that tell us the Holy Spirit's gifts are not limited to clergy or graduate students or certain certified people. Paul's teaching is either fanciful and merely another random first-century letter or it is revelatory: "To each is given the manifestation of the Spirit for the common good" (1 Corinthians 12:7). He uses the Greek word *ekastos*, a strong word that emphasizes the point: *to each and every one* is given the Spirit. It confirms what he told another congregation: "There is no longer Jew or Greek, there is no longer slave or free, there is no longer male and female; for all of you are one in Christ"(Galatians 3:28). If he was telling the truth, then we are in good hands within the body of Christ, the priesthood of amateurs, gifted by the Spirit and called to the whole range of ministries we need.

Styles of Mentoring

Gordon Shea understands that that mentoring takes many forms. He created the simple grid below around two elements: how structured or informal is the mentoring, and how short-term or long-term the duration?[1]

Highly structured, short-term	Highly structured, long-term
Informal, short-term	Informal, long-term

This simple graphic outlines a diverse set of practices or formats for spiritual mentoring.

- Spiritual mentoring may be highly structured and long term. Ignatius of Loyola created practices that included retreats, structured and long-term sessions for individual spiritual direction. The advantages of this format are many: typically no one is in a hurry to bring short-term results, and structure creates an expectation of a more authoritative and direct format and possibly includes a formal covenant.

- Some practice spiritual direction that is highly structured but is short term or possibly even situational as a person needs help through a particular season or life or circumstance.

- Spiritual mentoring may be long term but informal. This is practiced by some who contract with people for a longer-term process in a less formal and hierarchical format.

- Many experience in friendships what can be called spontaneous and mutual spiritual mentoring that is informal and short term.

The forms of mentoring are many. Is there a single correct form of direction or mentoring? No. Is the highly trained and highly structured spiritual director more skilled than the informally trained but deeply spiritual and careful reader of a life's story? Not necessarily. The debate about definitions can cause us to miss the larger point: we need others to come alongside us, and we can find help in many places, people and forms. Some are certified and have been carefully trained in spirituality, theology and psychology. Some are not formally trained but may be equally gifted in the school of life and uniquely skilled. As an academic dean I had to write a letter to the State of Washington every year to authorize a professor in our school to teach a course on spiritual direction. He did not have a doctorate in his field; in fact, he "only" had a BA in an unrelated field. He was, and in my mind still is, one of the most gifted spiritual directors I know. He is uniquely gifted to teach spirituality but required permission and authorization from the state in our credit-granting programs. Annoyed by the process but excited for the outcome, I wrote my letter each year to the Higher Education Commission to argue the case that Tom is distinctively and uniquely qualified for this work.

5

Imperfect People as Mentors

𝒟

Louie Zamperini didn't intend to become a world-class runner. He didn't expect to be the one who might break the four-minute mile. Born in 1917 as the child of Italian immigrants, he was, from the beginning, a wild child, constantly involved with "rough boys," often leading them to steal, fight, and provoke parents, teachers, police and anyone else in his way. And so he started to run, escaping by train boxcars and hitchhiking to Los Angeles. His brother, Pete, believed Louie to be a young man of great talent and potential and talked an angry school principal into letting Louie stay in school and run track. Chased by train detectives at gunpoint, he returned home and started to run track and then cross-country. With discipline he discovered himself capable of breaking school, state and national records, moving on to compete in the 1936 Olympics. His story is told in the book *Unbroken: A World War II Story of Survival, Resilience and Redemption*.[1] In 1941 he joined the Army, and in 1943 while searching for a missing aircraft, his plane crashed in the Pacific. Floundering for weeks on a life raft, he was eventually captured by the Japanese and endured the brutality of their prison camps until his eventual freedom and return home over two years later.

He is considered a true American hero. For me, however, the other hero in his story is his sixteen-year-old brother Pete, who believed in Louie and fought for him. After failing in school and being caught robbing it, Louie's future looked grim. But Pete argued that Louie could turn his life around. He believed in him even when the evidence was to the contrary.

One of my favorite pieces of pottery was given to me by a student early in my work in campus ministry. It was part of her "failure collection," she said. In the heating and refining process, what she envisioned as a perfect and beautiful bowl collapsed into a misshapen, miscolored object unlikely to be useful and certainly lacking in beauty. She gave it to me because we had talked about harsh and traumatic moments of abuse in her life. We talked about what felt like her failure and shame. Like Louie, she also had a champion, someone who helped her find redemption as she overcame tragedy in her life. As a mentor I had the sacred honor of standing alongside her to help her recast the way she read her story. Instead of a narrative about her failure, shame and trauma, we talked about abuse, beauty and redemption. In time, she read her narrative as words of hope and restoration and not only as heartbreak.

Mentors are not heroes or intentional champions, but they are those who will stand alongside another with unending curiosity, inexplicable faith and patience. You are reading this book quite likely because you are either seeking a mentor or are yourself a mentor. You want to know *how* this thing works. You want help to know if you are qualified, capable and ready for the holy work of mentoring. You might wonder if there are special qualities required for the work and training that will nurture any natural talents you might have. You may be surprised where preparation for mentoring needs to begin.

FAMILIAR WITH THE TRENCHES

Spiritual mentoring is not a boutique industry, something that is simply a luxury for a few with time, money and access. It is instead the equivalent of the battlefield. Mentoring is costly; it requires good recruitment, preparation and disciplined practice. There is a lot at stake. Read the fine print: while we are all mentors in a general sense, some of us have been recruited (called) for a ministry of mentoring with others. What kind of person is recruited for mentoring? What qualifications validate one's readiness for the ministry of mentoring? I think we dare not answer that question without reading Alan Jones's introduction to Margaret Guenther's book *Holy Listening*. He asks the question, "What kind of person, therefore, should be writing about the spiritual life today?" His answer:

> She would need to be very grounded in ordinary, everyday experience. She would need to be earthy and have the ability to see the funny side of the spiritual enterprise even in the midst of great suffering. She would need to be crafty—wily enough to spot the byzantine ploys of the ego to make itself the center of everything, even of its own suffering and struggle. She would need to be able to make judgments without being judgmental, to smell a rat without allowing her ability to discern deception sour her vision of the glory and joy that is everyone's birthright in God.[2]

The work of spirituality is about life in the trenches, on the battlefields and, sometimes, in the harshest things that life can bring. Preparation for mentoring begins in those trenches and battlefields. Spiritual mentoring is one way we fight the good fight of faith with companions on the journey. Sometimes it takes a ferocious resilience to make it through the day. In the last twenty-four hours I talked to people who faced severe crises: one is a colleague whose mother has fought brain cancer heroically for nearly a year. At the last exam, however, they told her the tumor was back now larger than before. It is now a matter of when, not if, she will die. Another stopped by to see her mother who stood in front of her toaster oven in tears and said, "I can't read the numbers anymore." Her impending blindness has darkened her world and will continue until she is completely sightless. A young friend, father of four, has just been informed his department has been downsized and he'll be unemployed within the month.

As mentors we come alongside, into places where the pain, grief and woundedness are indescribable. This is not work for casual observers, the faint of heart or the naively optimistic. So we do not come to the work of spiritual mentoring flippantly, casually or with a sense of superficiality. Read the fine print first. Anyone who desires to be a mentor to others must be willing to stand in another's soul with them—in whatever life in the trenches might bring.

Spiritual mentoring is learning to read the word written in the life of the mentee, to read what has been written in the story—all of it. Not only is God interested in the very best we bring, God has a long-time practice of using people whose lives lack integrity, coherence, faithfulness, grace, love, peace and obedience. Abraham lied freely. Jacob was the great deceiver. David was an adulterer who killed to protect his reputation. Saul/Paul was a violent man who sought to destroy Christians. Peter was one who betrayed Jesus in his greatest hour of need. The list is as long as the story of every hero of the faith. The more time we spend in Scripture the more we realize there really aren't *heroes* of faith; there are only ordinary people who sometimes have extraordinary experiences with God in the lifelong journey of many ordinary days and nights. They are people who are flawed and finite. Those aren't excuses for anyone;

they are honest words about every mentor, every mentee and everyone you know. They are people who have failed and tried to do better and have failed again. The live in repentance and redemption; they know grace because they have experienced it firsthand. Paul's insight in Romans 2 is breathtaking: "Do you not realize that God's kindness is meant to lead you to repentance?" (Romans 2:4). Not contempt and judgment, but kindness is God's present means of grace. Generosity, acts of consideration, benevolence, compassion and tenderness—these embody kindness.

TRAINED BY SCRIPTURE: DEVELOPING A SACRED HISTORICAL IMAGINATION

Learning to read biblical text is one of our best methods for preparing for life in the trenches because it equips us to read the narratives of our own lives. Reading biblical narratives requires historical imagination as we enter the stories of their lives. Reading the Bible is not a spectator sport. We engage the narrative and enter the story with sacred imagination. Rather than keeping it at arm's length, we embrace the humanity of the narrative. It prepares us for good mentoring.

Brennan Manning called us all "ragamuffins," a ragged band of ordinary people bound together by a common faith on a common journey. Paul, arguably the most influential apostle of all, was quick to declare himself "the greatest sinner of all." Why did he make that claim? Was it a preacher's ploy to create a bond with his audience? Was it rhetorical hyperbole? I don't think so. It was instead an honest assessment of his own story of faith. He knew he was a man flawed, failed, finite and very, very human. He knew he struggled with temptations, lust, anger, a desire for power and with his own private warfare with his soul. He also knew himself to be the recipient of grace. Those aren't words of empty rhetoric, but rather of a deeply honest understanding of our true nature. The culture of Christian faith for many in North America is the gated community of incomplete truth. We show each other our very best culturally approved self but not our fears, anger, deception, lust, anxiety, jealousy or pain. And yet, in my church, we confess all of this to God every week and hear the words spoken over us, "You are forgiven." The mentor will not be surprised to see in the stories of mentees echoes of biblical narratives. Mentoring is not only available for the good person who desires to get better but for all who long to grow. When it comes to our spiritual growth, we are all, always beginners.

The timeline for Christian growth is never a single line of upward progress. I can hear someone say, "If I am faithful, committed, disciplined and strong, can I not see steady, consistent and upward growth?" It sounds good but I don't know anyone who, if they're honest, has only experienced growth. Why? We live in a spiritual world, which Paul said includes "principalities and powers." "For our struggle is not against enemies of blood and flesh, but against the rulers, against the authorities, against the cosmic powers of this present darkness, against the spiritual forces of evil in the heavenly places" (Ephesians 6:12). There is an enemy, and there are forces that battle our progress. The powers are real. And the enemy knows us well enough to find our weaknesses and assault them.

In my church, preparation for the Eucharist requires prayers of confession for "what we have done and what we have left undone." The words are painfully comprehensive—it's hard to tell myself I have nothing to confess when it asks me what sin I have committed by action and inaction, lack of faith, failure to love, insipid compassion or unjust practices that I don't even remember on Sunday. Dallas Willard has said we practice faith until it is habituated within our lives. I hope he is right. I long for habits of holiness to characterize all of our lives. And I am grateful each week for the words of the rector who makes the sign of the cross over an entire congregation of confessed sinners and says, "Your sins have been forgiven you". . . until next time. The habit I believe in most fervently as essential to lasting spiritual growth is the habit of confession—for mentee and mentor alike. While the mentoring session is not typically a confessional, no part of our story is out of bounds.

THE SPIRITUALITY OF IMPERFECTION

Something happens when I open myself in transparent authenticity to tell my story to another. We move from casual conversationalists to coconspirators in the reading of life as story. We eavesdrop on the story unfolding in time and place. When I tell you my story, I invite you into the glory and the pain, the beauty and the shadows, the light and the dark. All of these are present where there is authentic storytelling because our lives are immersed in all of them. Richard Rohr calls it the spirituality of imperfection, or the "way of the wound."[3] To make sure we understand the true texture of life, he said, "Pain is part of the deal."[4] Those words did not match the spiritual training of my background. Mine was a spirituality of perfection, performance, achievement and production. Christian discipleship seemed very much like the Swedish cultural overlay of my life.

- "Do your best."
- "Don't draw attention to yourself."
- "Don't tell family secrets outside the home."
- "God loves you because you are trying very hard to do what is right."
- "When you fail, brush yourself off and get on with your life, but don't let it happen again."

Whatever family system you were raised in, you perceived messages, cultural mores and heartbreak. My life was marked from before my birth by the birth of a firstborn child, my brother, who was tragically brain damaged in birth. For the four children who followed his birth, the die was cast. This family was structured around behaviors that made things work for an emotionally challenged oldest child. There came a natural stifling of loud outbursts, active behaviors or emotional displays that could upset him and create further trauma for everyone. Television shows were monitored so as not to upset or rile up Jerry. Add a very conservative theological framework of external, behavior-driven spirituality and you can imagine the story of my life. The goal was control and perfection, or at least the appearance of it. I came to believe that God is irritated and suspicious of us most of the time because we don't perform at the highest level at all times. What emerged was a spirituality of perfection, performance and production. As a result, the most frightened people I know never understood their own imperfection so they never learned from the most important teachers of all: heartbreak, brokenness, shadows and woundedness. These are the spiritual teachers whose classroom we are wise to return to often, but that was not the case in my life until I had to face the reality of my inability to perform, be perfect and produce; not so until I faced the walls of limitations and the abyss of imperfection. The problem is that most of the people in my world were shaped by that same kind of spirituality so I needed to find mentors who had spent time in the trenches of heartbreak.

Rather than keeping Scripture at arm's length, the mentor embraces the humanity of the narrative. It prepares us for mentoring. Gratefully I began to find mentors in Scripture like Paul, to whom God said, "My grace is sufficient for you, for power is made perfect in weakness" (2 Corinthians 12:9). Because he understood that, Paul was able to say, "So, I will boast all the more gladly of my weaknesses, so that the power of Christ may dwell in me. Therefore I am content with weaknesses, insults, hardships, persecutions, and calamities for the sake of Christ; for whenever I am weak, then I am strong" (2 Corinthians 12:9-10). It was this same Paul who also confessed, "For I do not do the good I want, but the evil I do not want is what I do" (Romans 7:19). With such honesty, arguably the greatest of the apostles looked into his own soul and saw his desperate need for grace. I wasn't raised to think of biblical mentors and teachers being described in such words. But I found them when I needed to know that they were as human and flawed as I. And gradually I found other mentors who invited me to sit in the shadows and the wounds because they knew that freedom, life and healing are found in those stories, and not only in the stories of victory and success. We don't get to choose only glory, beauty and victory; our need for mentors is marked by our own trauma, shame, abuse and failure.

> But we have this treasure in clay jars, so that it may be made clear that this extraordinary power belongs to God and does not come from us. We are afflicted in every way, but not crushed; perplexed, but not driven to despair; persecuted, but not forsaken; struck down, but not destroyed. . . . So death is at work in us, but life in you. (2 Corinthians 4:7-9, 12)

Because of this text, N. T. Wright called the human family "battered old flowerpots filled with the glory of God" and said, "The church is called to be where the world is in pain, at the place where the world is suffering and in a state of shame and sorrow. The church is there as the presence of the suffering Christ in the world."[5] I used to believe that was the heroic or martyr-like behavior of the few action figure–type Christians or leaders who could stand above the fray and call others to follow them to the place of perfection they had somehow achieved. The trouble is, I don't know anyone like that. I know good people, dedicated people, honorable people and even a few whose lives have inspired me as exemplars, but I don't know any who don't have feet of clay. Brandi Carlyle's song "The Story" says it in one line: "All of these lines across my face tell you the story of who I am." We are marred and marked by life; for Jesus, it was his hands and feet that carried his scars. Where is it for you?

LIVING IN DAILY TRUST

Brennan Manning wrote a prayer to the living Lord that captures the sine qua non in the qualification of any mentor. They believe deeply in God and know their own deep and daily need for God's hand to be on their life, God's voice to be heard in their life and God's forgiveness to be given daily in their own experience.

> Abba, into your hands I entrust my body, mind and spirit and this entire day—morning, afternoon, evening and night. Whatever you want of me, *I* want of me, falling into you and trusting in you in the midst of my life. Into your heart I entrust my heart, feeble, distracted, insecure, uncertain. Abba, unto you I abandon myself in Jesus our Lord, Amen.[6]

If that prayer seems too easy, you never knew Brennan. A former Catholic priest, professor and theologian, Brennan was also an embattled alcoholic. Even as he spoke to crowds of people eager to learn about how to be a ragamuffin or Abba's child, he battled his addiction to the end it seemed. He knew the need to live one day at a time in his battle with alcohol but, more deeply, to know himself forgiven as a failed and flawed human being. He was not only a voice of grace to us all, he was the presence of God in the trenches.

In a particularly dark and hard time in my spiritual journey, I was in frequent conversation with Brennan, who confronted me one night in a phone call as I lamented my struggles and confessed my sin. "Your problem, Keith, is that you are a minor-league sinner. Compared to me, your sin is in the bush leagues. But your greater problem is that you haven't yet learned to receive the richness of grace that is offered. You stay in your lament over your sin because you are ego-centered." The words were comical at first and then confrontational to hear. I thought it was "spiritual" to name sin and confess my failures. I thought it was an act of spiritual humility to honestly declare myself a sinner. Brennan knew that grace is what it's about. "I live in mercy, and I live in today." Those words from him have never left me. Mercy is a daily gift, given because I am in need of forgiveness every day. It is given but some, like me, are loathe to receive it because we choose instead to dwell in the darkness of our worst self rather than in the possibility of our true self—the forgiven self. The mentor who brings what the mentee needs is one who knows sin and forgiveness, darkness and light, failure and transformation. The mentor is not someone who has mastered all things spiritual as much as someone who knows about starting over in faith every single day. And the mentor knows how to sit comfortably in the presence of each of these.

Effective mentors are honest about their own brokenness and the holes within. They don't impose those on others, but they practice the art of mentoring with a whole canvas and not only landscapes of sunrise and beauty. And they are not surprised by the brokenness of their mentees. The mentor does not sit in judgment on another; they are truth-tellers who offer a pathway to re-demption. Perhaps that's why some of my best mentors have lived long enough to know their own story in many chapters. A spiritu-ality of imperfection acknowledges the chapters of failure, harm and suffering and the chapters of repentance and redemption. As only she can say, Anne Lamott proposes we're all alike in one way: "Everyone is screwed up, broken, clingy, and scared, even the people who seem to have it more or less together. They are much more like you than you would believe. So try not to compare your insides to their outsides. Also, you can't save, fix or rescue any of them, or get any of them sober."[7] I would like to dismiss her words as irreverent or banal, but the problem is they echo biblical texts that we are alike in our brokenness. In my evangelical childhood, we reserved those thoughts only for those who had "once been lost" but "now were found," not those who are still lost and seeking.

It makes a difference if you believe Scripture is telling the truth about our nature and if you believe it applies to you. One of the haunting questions I have been asked is, "Do you actually know anyone who lives the kind of spirituality you're talking about?" Those words were leveled against the kind of perfection that I was taught to desire. I was also taught that you can't let up on seeking holiness or you might lose your edge to fight creeping imperfection. Like Lamott, however, I've lived too long to believe that. My failures qualify me to read my own story of grace, healing and re-demption. My confessions qualify me to know forgiveness for myself and to long for it for others. My imperfection qualifies me to turn my face to Jesus, the only one who is the author and finisher of my faith. My experience of grace qualifies me to tell the story of redemption and forgiveness.

PERFECT PEOPLE NEED NOT APPLY

So I say: Don't set out to be a mentor unless you know yourself to be a person of human failure and the recipient of grace. You may not want to hear that, but it is profoundly important. Most of us aren't looking for mentors who believe they are better than the rest of us or in being coached by the NFL pro-bowl star. I want someone who has lived the struggle—more like an Alcoholics Anonymous sponsor—knowing they are capable of the slip that leads to the fall. I have known some of the best; I no longer demand perfection from them but humility in their humanity. Mentors who ignore such words or believe they are beyond them need not apply. The mentors who are worthy of emulation are those who still smell the failure and taste the sweetness of forgiveness because it is fresh every day. Like Paul, they are our best teachers of redemption.

My early encounter with mentoring was with a professor who had experienced a nervous breakdown as a young postgraduate student. I didn't know that part of his story until three years into our relationship, but I always felt the presence of it. I could tell he had been changed, fundamentally transformed, by some experience in his life because he spoke with a confident humility. The words sound contradictory, don't they? But he was a man who had been humbled by his encounter with his humanity, and he was confident that he had faced the worst and weakest parts of himself with the grace of God. Not the shallow triumphalism that gloats about victory over sin but rather an honest, face-to-face encounter with his own soul. He taught me to be more honest than I knew how to be. Honest about those things that I couldn't speak of freely in all settings. Honest about questions, doubts, longings, fears and ambivalence. Honest about moments lived with faith and moments lived without faith. Honest about my struggle to pray and my inability to practice the very things I taught others.

Eugene Peterson defines spiritual formation succinctly: "Spiritual formation is primarily what the Spirit does, forming the resurrection life of Christ in us."[8] Imitate me, therefore, as you see places and ways that God the Holy Spirit has formed Christlikeness in me. Imitate me in the ways you and others see Christ living in me. Listen with me to the voice of Spirit in our times together. And what about the rest? Learn from me; be instructed by my mistakes; grow from my failures; be encouraged by the forgiveness I have been given; join me in the lifelong cycle of true discipleship, persistence and rebirth. To whom did Jesus say, "You must be born again?" It was to the religious leader and teacher Nicodemus, the one who spent his life teaching others about the life of faith. The life of faith is like physical health: you don't get healthy once and for all time; it takes a lifetime of disciplines and practices, nurture, nutrition and exercise.

In mentoring, all of life is available material for teaching. If there is anything I want to broadcast as loudly as I can it is that we learn to read our story through the Holy Spirit only as we learn to read *all* of our story and place it willingly before God. I have found my failures provide the best times of growth and formation. My pain has taught me more than my success. My times of greatest vulnerability came in my times of greatest success, I believe, because I stopped paying attention. My heartbreaks have shown me plots and subplots that I would rather deny or compartmentalize into protected, almost gated parts of my soul. I much prefer to read the narratives of success, joy, glory, delight, contentment and celebration. I much prefer the seasons of orientation to seasons of disorientation, but there is much to be learned from pain, brokenness and failure.

Spiritual Mentoring as
Cura Animarum

The English phrase "care of souls" has its origins in the Latin *cura animarum*. While *cura* is most commonly translated "care," it actually contains the idea of both care and cure.

- Care refers to actions designed to support the well-being of something or someone.

- Cure refers to actions designed to restore well-being that has been lost.[1]

All spiritual formation work includes both building and repair. No one grows without broken places or pain. The care of souls takes place only where there is honest attention to your own failure and pain. That's why leaders in Christian organizations are some of the neediest people on the planet when it comes to spiritual formation. We're too busy, too important, too much in front, too depended on, too prideful, and we live too much in the safety of our silos. Many leaders I know want to learn to do the work of the care of souls for others when they are deeply in need of care and cure for their own souls.

The care of the soul has always involved four primary elements:

- Healing (restoring to health from impairment)
- Sustaining (helping one to endure and transcend circumstances)
- Reconciling (broken relationships)
- Guiding (helping one to make wise decisions)[2]

Writing many years ago, Richard Baxter's words still need to be heard: Start with yourself and take heed of your own spiritual vulnerability. "See that the work of saving grace be thoroughly wrought in your own souls. Take heed to yourselves, lest you be void of that saving grace of God which you offer to others, and be strangers to the effectual working of that gospel which you preach."[3] Who is most in need of the special care of cura animarum? Baxter's list may surprise you.

1. The spiritually weak or those in need

2. Those with a special "handicap," by which he meant a physical or spiritual addiction, including pride

3. The tempted (to worldliness, gluttony, drunkenness, and so on)

4. The disconsolate (or subject to emotional depression)

5. The strong. When we believe ourselves to be strong, we may believe we have earned our success because we are especially talented, gifted or distinctly skilled, when in fact, we have been blessed.[4]

To all leaders, pastors, mentors, and writers he would say, "Take heed to yourselves."[5] This was the hardest for me to handle. On the one hand he wanted me to identify the places where I lived as an imposter—to fearlessly name the lies I told myself and the lies I lived before others. But on the other hand, he wanted me to befriend myself. He said pointedly, "Get over yourself."

Part Two

Uncovering the Movements of the Spiritual Mentoring Relationship

6

Starting Well

Finally, some readers will say, we've landed the plane. At last we can get to the nuts and bolts—the mechanics of mentoring. However, mentoring reduced to mechanics becomes a formula or checklist of questions, as if each person fits into a one-size-fits-all set of clothing.

Scientists who study the human eye tell us each eye is as distinctive as a human fingerprint; no two are alike. Therapists learn to listen to each person in ways that respect their distinctiveness and individuality. No story is the same in the life of two people. Some even point out that the childhood experience of siblings is not the same; after all, parents relate differently to a boy than a girl or to an older child than a younger child. The life situation of the parents changes as children grow up and the family moves through different stages. The age of parents can add other developmental differences. In the same way, no two mentoring experiences are alike.

When we create a simplistic protocol for every person we run the risk of reductionism. Mentoring may follow repeatable methods from person to person, but it is more than a simple formula. Mentoring requires an almost inexhaustible curiosity to listen to the story that now sits alongside you. I use those words on purpose. You listen to a person who is, herself or himself, a story. They bring a story that is not the same as the one they brought a week or a month before. Why? They have lived life and their character has developed in that time; plot lines have unfolded, and God has been at work in the minutes, hours, days and weeks.

There is a rush to adopt methods and technology in North American culture in general and in church culture in particular. We want to know *how*, when instead we need to learn from Jesus about taking time with *what* and *why*. Think about it. Where and how did Jesus define his most important teaching about the kingdom of God or reign of God? Jesus didn't define kingdom of God or kingdom of heaven at all, at least not in the way our technological culture prefers. He didn't do it as an academic exercise, which typically starts with definition of terms. And he didn't do it as a guide with an overview and a map of the terrain. He started where he needs us to begin: with stories, parables and metaphors. The kingdom of God is like

- a father who loses a son, a woman who loses a coin, a shepherd who loses a sheep

- a woman imploring a judge to listen

- a door, a gate, a boss, a merchant

- a tiny seed, a farmer who sows, a rescuer of a robbery/assault and a fruitless fig tree

- a pearl of great price, a treasure, cloth, new wine skins, a dinner, a rich man

- bread from heaven, water, wine, the washing of feet

As with much of his teaching, he was indirect and suggestive rather than definitive. He told parables that made you think and wonder. He used metaphors that weren't easily understood. He asked questions whose answers weren't always what the listeners wanted to hear. In theology we say that Jesus used analogical language—the language of comparison—to call us to see. Did you know the Greek word for *parable* comes from two words that mean "a throwing down alongside"? The parable is the essential language of analogy. Great teachers have always found ways to suggest, evoke, provoke and draw out response from others. "Education" comes from Latin words meaning to educe, to draw forth meaning. Why then would mentoring be different? Why would it be formulaic, methodical and mechanical?

And yet there are predictable movements in the process—to start well the mentor needs to have some idea of the movements of mentoring. Not steps in a linear Gantt chart, but perhaps a flow of movements through the living relationship of mentor and mentee. In its simplest form, the movements of mentoring are starting well, sustaining well and ending well. In this chapter we focus on starting well.

STARTING WELL: INQUIRY, INTERVIEW AND INTAKE

Mentoring is initiated by prayerful discernment. There is a cycle of events that most simply describe the movements of starting well. These aren't a checklist of steps; rather, I have come to think of them as movements.

1. *Inquiry* is when a mentee or mentor initiates and inquires about the prospect of working together in mentoring. It is a movement toward discernment. This may be an informal conversation after a meeting, worship time, class or chance conversation. It may be as simple as, "Can we grab some coffee and talk?" The point is also simple: it starts with one person taking a step toward another. This is prompted by the Holy Spirit, but it often feels like a stuttering step. It is

simply an act of taking initiative to start the conversation. It is often a casual, seemingly random conversation that leads to something more.

2. *Interview* is one way to speak of a first meeting that explores the possibility of starting mentoring together. It is helpful to think of this conversation as an interview by both mentor and mentee. The dynamic is one of exploration: Are we a good fit for the intentional work of mentoring together? What do we need to know about each other? An interview is a two-way street—both ask and answer; both speak and listen. It will likely include prayer and a commitment to wait and discern. It is not yet the first formal meeting.

3. *Intake* is a first session that starts the actual work of mentoring. Formal or informal, the mentor takes the lead and focuses on at least three essentials:

- Mentors set expectations and calibrate the pace.

- Mentors set agreements for how the work will proceed. It is intentional and may lead to the development of a covenant. Because mentoring is scheduled and accountable, agreements are set for frequency of meetings and practices of accountability.

- Agreements are set for the duration of the mentoring process and for assessment during the process itself. Most mentoring sessions last about an hour and may be weekly or monthly. Some, however, find ways to meet for half-day "retreats" or even whole weekends quarterly or semi-annually. Duration, frequency and length of sessions are adapted to fit the availability and needs of the mentee.

WHERE CAN GOOD MENTORS BE FOUND?

In a course on spiritual mentoring, I assigned students an exercise of finding a prospective mentor so they could at least taste the mentoring experience. I was curious as I waited to see how their search would go. Some had it easy. They had prospects in their church or workplace, in a small group, or in their larger kinship groups. In other words, they knew people who might have an inclination, interest or even calling for the work. Others were frustrated as they soon realized their relative isolation as new students in a new setting. Soon, however, they identified someone from their past who they could ask; some were older family members, former teachers or professors, coaches, pastors, church elders or even mentors from an earlier season of life. Many students turned to spiritual friends who were ready to explore the ministry of mentoring along with the prospective mentee.

On some occasions mentors are assigned. I find those to be the least effective, though not always. Rather than google "spiritual mentor" in a local community, mentees will need to explore their current and past circle of relationships. It is not always an easy task. In many cases it is a matter of taking the risk to ask someone who is new to them. I've done it both with success and without.

BEFORE WE BEGIN: INQUIRY AND DISCERNMENT

We might say that mentoring begins before the beginning. Before you schedule session one, both mentor and mentee need to practice prayerful discernment. The timeline doesn't start with your inquiry; it already started in the heart of God. You've read this before: mentoring starts with God. Your part is to discern what God intends. That's why our hunger for technology can be damaging to our spiritual development. The more we take our spiritual development into our own hands and believe it depends on us, the more likely we are to impede the growth that God intends. One question is most pertinent in the discernment process. As a prospective mentee, ask yourself the questions Jesus asked: "What are you looking for?" (John 1:38). It is the great question of discernment. "Why do you believe mentoring will be helpful to you?" Honestly asked, it may bring to light mistaken reasons we seek out a mentor.

- Sometimes we're looking for a human messiah who will become the one who saves us from loneliness, confusion or fear. We mistakenly are looking for someone who can fix us.

- Sometimes we're looking for someone who can actually help us avoid asking the hard questions ourselves. We push that responsibility off to the mentor believing he or she will know more or know better than I do or help me defer the hard questions I need to ask.

- Sometimes the desire to be mentored is an impulsive act in response to a class, blog, sermon or experience. Spiritual mentoring is a discipline that will require time and commitment from both mentor and mentee; it requires wise listening and not simply a knee-jerk reaction or impulse. This impulse can either lead to good work or an abrupt closure. Mentoring requires intentionality and commitment to put in the time.

- Sometimes we think someone else can give us an answer we're seeking. Jesus' response to John's disciple urges a different path. "Come and see" is his invitation to practice the spirituality of attention. Most of the "answers" are within, awaiting a process of discovery.

The mentee undertakes to ask God for guidance to find a mentor. The nature of spiritual mentoring is to listen well together, and listening starts with the selection of a mentor. Urgency by a mentee can be a warning sign. Without discernment, motivation is questionable. Ask God as simply and directly as you can, "Who do you have in mind for me?" The prospective mentor may say no because their load is full, their focus is elsewhere or their sense of connection with the mentee is not compelling. So the mentee knocks on another door. If you remember any advice from this book, remember this: you may need to be persistent in your search for a mentor. Keep looking even if you are turned down by prospective mentors. God intends for you to walk alongside another in this holy work of reading your life.

For the prospective mentor, the inquiry and interview process can be a time of temptation.

- We may be tempted by the ego rush of being asked to be a mentor.

- We may be tempted by the authority rush when another person seeks us out.

- We are sometimes tempted by our own inability to say no.

Each of these is seductive and intoxicating. Discernment before answering is a sacred task. The most important thing we will give as we begin is honest discernment and time. The form this question takes for the mentor is "What am I able and willing to bring to this relationship?"

So before we start the work of mentoring, we begin with discernment to confirm that now is the time for mentoring with this particular person. It's not complicated; pray, listen and wait. Only then should you start. Inquiry is the movement of initiation; we start somewhere.

In my life, some mentoring relationships have been initiated by the mentor and some by the mentee. Someone tapped me on the shoulder once and said, "You need to come and see me," so I

did. That started a three-year mentoring process. In another circumstance, I was the one to knock on the door to ask someone
to mentor me. As it turns out, my first spiritual mentor was assigned to me at a conference. Other spiritual mentors have been
peers, older and younger; clergy; and laity, certified and not. I
have asked and been denied by several who felt they were not
qualified, ready or "worthy." I have been sought out by only a
handful, who turned out to be some of my best. I have had seasons
of both formal and informal mentoring and, sadly, a season or
two, without.

Who initiates is less important than that a connection is
created between the two. Call it chemistry, empathy or a vibe,
but there needs to be some connection that draws two people
together. That's why I follow a common practice when someone
requests that I mentor him or her. I wait. My first response to a
prospective mentee is discernment. I will almost certainly delay
giving an answer while I take time to pray about the possibility
of starting this relationship. I will then be honest about the following questions:

- Why mentoring? What is this person looking for?

- Why me? Why did they choose to ask me to mentor them?
  What role might I play in their life?

- Why now? What has prompted their search for a mentor at this
  moment in their life?

- Why not? Are there issues, concerns, red flags or even yellow
  caution flags for us to enter a mentoring relationship? Do we
  have history, good or bad? Is the individual realistic about what
  mentoring can mean? Are there any reasons, circumstantial or
  personal, that would lead me to say no?

THE INTERVIEW

The word *interview* might conjure images of something formal—a job interview, a news reporter asking questions or an insurance adjustor gathering information. However, the interview is simply a time for the prospective mentor and mentee to meet and talk about expectations. When it comes to this meeting, the phrase "What you see is what you get" speaks an important truth. Our expectations can shape our experiences. We both expand and limit possibilities based on what we expect to see.

Climbing to Little Tahoma, the 11,138-foot peak southeast of the summit of Mount Rainier, the group I was with started out at the White River Campground. I knew the route would take us across Frying Pan Glacier. The name does not create confidence in any savvy mountaineer. It was, however, precisely what I expected. On a blazing hot August day, we trudged across the nearly flat plateau of snow at about eight thousand feet, utterly exposed to the blinding reflection of sun against snow. I was grateful to be prepared with clown white lotion that protected my nose from sunburn, climbing glasses to keep my eyes from the same pain of sunburn and shorts to make the temperature bearable. The repetition of training under our guide and leader, Leroy, shaped our expectations.

In mentoring, as in most ministry, the work isn't always easily described in simple terms. The "technology" of mentoring is fairly direct and simple: it's all about listening—to the Spirit and to the mentee. But that's where the simplicity ends. Like any Alpine hike, each trek is different than the one before. It's not only weather and conditions that change, but the terrain itself, while familiar, is different. The snow depth and thickness changes, the crevasses open and close on the surface, and the hardness of snow, ice and glacial snow pack can be different every time. It is important to shape expectations in preparation for the climb. Spiritual mentoring starts best when it orients the mentee to the reflective work that lies ahead. If mentees are looking for a consumer-based experience that will give them a jolt for the week or the promise of a stirring emotional shot, they might want to try something else. Spiritual mentoring can be slow, reflective, quiet, repetitive, awkward and stuttering, just like the rest of your life. In the interview stage, mentor and mentee begin to articulate answers to the underlying question: What are you looking for?

Rather than start at the beginning, perhaps we are best helped to start at the end: What is the intended outcome of the work? What can one expect from mentoring? The outcome is that you will live life. I am not trying to be clever but honest. After years of mentoring and spiritual direction, I have lived life and sometimes known myself alive and attuned to the Spirit of God. I have grown in faith and, I believe, in righteousness, but not always in an upward arcing line. Two steps forward, three steps back. But I have lived life. I know myself with keener insights at times; I love more deeply than I once did, and I listen for the kingdom with ears trained to listen and eyes trained to see. I look for the kingdom more often than I once did and in less predictable places and times than I once did because I know it remains an elusive and hidden reality. But this is not always true of me. The deadly sins can grip my life just as they do everyone else. The goal is to be a person marked by the fruit of the Spirit: "Love, joy, peace, patience, kindness, generosity, faithfulness, gentleness, and self-control" (Galatians 5:22-23). I approach the sacred task of giving spiritual direction with great humility and a daily experience of grace.

THE INTAKE SESSION

An intake session often gets specific as it sets expectations, pace, schedule, and accountability. Counselors, physicians and social workers use a first session as an intake session to gather data, diagnose information and create a treatment plan. While it may sound clinical, the mentoring intake is simply a first meeting. Mentors use an intake session to create intentionality, set expectations and develop pace. Mentors also use an intake session to discuss details of schedule, location and accountability. Intentionality marks the mentoring relationship as different from spiritual friendship. During the intake session, the mentor and mentee make a commitment to the conversation and prayerfully consider it. I like to start with an agreement to meet four times and then assess.

Some have an intake protocol that uses a simple spiritual biography: "Describe what you consider the spiritual development of your life" or "Describe your spiritual journey as a chronology of your life from childhood to the present." I have used a prayer history, which asks the mentee to describe seasons of prayer in his or her life, including neglect or absence of prayer. In my work in premarital counseling I use a simplistic analogy for my time with the couple. "Just start somewhere, because your relationship is a bit like a piece of pie. It contains some of the layers of all parts of your life. As we work our way through various layers, we are able to dig into the complex nuance of your lives." It is the same in mentoring.

The tone is contemplative and reflective. Wherever it begins, expect thoughtful conversation, good questions and gaps of silence. Your task as mentor is not to keep a conversation going, it is to invite reflective conversation. Don't be surprised by pauses, silence, uncertainty and hesitant responses. Lively conversations can be marked by reflective silence. Mentees need to anticipate slow conversation and see it as progress. The mentee is not there to give answers but to enter a holy space and listen. Some of us are not used to being listened to well. Some of us are not used to leisurely, contemplative reflection. We fill the space with words when silence and pause may be enough. Some of us are not comfortable sitting in silence with another; the wise mentor will invite experiments in silence starting with only a minute or two and building to longer spaces. "Let's take two minutes to sit together and reflect on the question. It's important, and good questions need time. We're not in a hurry."

Whether a covenant is written formally or discussed informally, an intake session will discuss expectations for both mentor and mentee. After a time of inquiry and interview, set the first meeting and begin the conversation. Show up and get started. Many mentees come to a first session without a clear sense of what will occur but often with high expectations for something important to happen. Just as good therapist will ask, "What brings you here?" so the mentor starts with expectations. The first session may include an orientation to the spirituality of attention and listening. It isn't unusual to start with the list of "what spiritual mentoring isn't" so mentees can adjust their expectations. The process starts with a first conversation. It doesn't need to be complicated or even called mentoring—it can be as simple as lunch or coffee. The progression to week two and beyond is shaped by intentionality.

There is always the danger of misguided or inflated expectations, which move the mentoring process off-course. Spiritual mentoring is not

- a pulpit for the mentor's sermonizing with a captive audience (the mentee)

- a therapy couch where the mentor treats problems or resolves issues for the mentee

- a vending machine where the mentor dispenses wisdom "on demand"
- a white board where the mentor strategizes solutions for the problem of the day for the mentee
- a dispensary for giving answers to the question of the day
- a pharmacy to distribute cures and health-giving elixirs
- a travel agency with a ticket to escape the day-to-day and year-to-year
- a life guard chair at the beach to save those who are in danger
- a classroom for instruction in a pre-determined curriculum of Christlikeness
- a voice-activated feature on your smartphone to give you GPS-like directions for your travels
- a chapter from my life imposed on the narrative of another
- a handbook of ten steps to the accomplished spiritual life
- an orchestra score with completed compositions for harmony, beauty and melody

So, my starting place with mentees is to set expectations that are low. I know that sounds negative to some, but one of my mentors often says that spirituality is the slowest of all speeds. We want to move ahead quickly and accelerate often, as if we are entering the onramp to a freeway; in reality, however, there is no onramp for high speed, but rather the slow, deliberate speed of growing seeds, cultivating fruit and waiting for a harvest that will one day come. What should we expect from the sacred work of mentoring?

- We will proceed wisely and with intentionality.
- We will set a pace that is productive and possible for both of us and not only for one.

- We will cultivate a relationship more than a procedure.
- We will allow space for silence and not rush to fill the space with words.
- We will learn patience with one another and with the Spirit.
- We will learn to trust each other and the Spirit.
- We will practice honest words with each other.
- We will expect presence and blessing . . . in God's good time.
- We will learn mutually in giving and receiving.
- We will make room for leisurely and deliberate conversation.
- We will celebrate small moments of insight, wisdom and discernment.

CREATING A COVENANT OF AGREEMENTS

Some mentors create a mentoring covenant. This excellent tool asks all of the essential questions for the mentor and mentee to start well. Covenant making was a time-honored practice in the ancient world. God created covenants with people like Noah, Abraham, Moses and David. Each covenant was an agreement between Yahweh and either a person or a people. It specified certain understandings between Yahweh and people and contained promises made mutually. Covenant making is one of the ways God offered a relationship of intimacy to people under the old covenant and through Jesus in the new covenant (New Testament). The biblical practice of covenant making offers a practical tool for the early stage of the mentoring relationship. A mentoring covenant is a simple written or verbal agreement between the mentor and mentee. It is best arranged around three categories:

1. *Philosophical.* What do we hope to do in these sessions? What are we looking for? What has prompted the mentee to seek out a mentor? What agreements do we have about confidentiality? Will we publicly acknowledge the mentoring work in the presence of others?

2. *Logistical.* Where will we meet? For how long? What will create maximum comfort and safety for the mentee? Should another staff person be present in an office nearby rather than meeting in an isolated office space? How will cell phones be allowed? Some mentees need cell phone availability for children or elder care. Will there be assignments or exercises of accountability?

3. *Closure.* How will we know we have completed the work?

Covenant making moves the soul friendship of good friends into the soul work of spiritual mentoring. In some cases, friends are capable of being mentors to one another, but the intentionality of a covenant elevates expectations for both. In some situations, the added question is one of cost. Is there a fee for spiritual mentoring that needs to be negotiated by mentor and mentee as they begin their work? For some, mentoring is purely a generous gift of time; for others, spiritual direction is a ministry of private practice.

Spiritual Mentoring
as Disillusionment

I love to study the meaning of words. One of my most prized books is called *Origins: A Short Etymological Dictionary of Modern English*, written by Eric Partridge. Etymology basically studies the origin of words in Latin, Greek, Old English or elsewhere. It shows how words change over time and how their meaning evolves as culture shapes the way we use words. As I set out to write or prepare for classes, speeches or presentations, I open the Partridge book to learn about a word I intend to use. It happened a while ago as I intended to use the word illusion. Partridge says the word originated in a combination of words that share a common origin with ludicrous, which means to mock.[1] An illusion is a distortion or a false picture of what we thought was true. Our eyes deceived us; our ears got it wrong.

And then I found Barbara Brown Taylor's use of the word disillusionment and was caught off guard. To disillusion is to effectively remove or replace one's illusions. What we take for granted and believe to be the way things are in the world has become an illusion in our own worldviews of thought.

Disillusioned, we find that God does not conform to our expectations. We glimpse our own relative size in the universe and see that no human being can say who God should be or how God should act. We review our requirements of God and recognize them as our own fictions, things we tell ourselves to make ourselves feel safe or good or comfortable. Disillusioned, we find out what is not true and we are set free to seek what is—if we dare—to turn away from the God who was supposed to be in order the seek the God who is.[2]

Mentoring as disillusionment is a surprising metaphor. But disillusionment, it turns out, can be a good thing. The mentor assists the mentee to replace an illusion with something that is more substantively true, accurate, or "real." It's often been said that we have a true self and a false self, created from distorted ways of seeing, remembering and thinking. In mentoring, we often help a mentee replace the illusion of a false self with a true self. Most often, it is to replace the dominating illusion of guilt, shame and brokenness for a new vision of self as beloved, forgiven, redeemed and healed. Brennan Manning once challenged me to seek out the roles of the imposter in my life. He said I wasn't much good at it. "Transparency," he wisely told me, "is a supreme act of trust in God." I agreed with him; that sounded accurate. But then he lowered the boom: "Keith, you practice self-deception rather than transparency." It wasn't that I was surprised by his observation; it was the brutal honesty and directness of his words that disillusioned me. "When you truly befriend yourself and your spiritual depth, and the miraculous movement of the Spirit to make you the man you are today, as you affirm that goodness, you don't need the approval of others."

To dis-illusion requires the courage to tell the mentee the truth as you know it. To dis-illusion requires a steady reading of Scripture to know the mind and heart of God. Otherwise we will impose our own illusion in place of truth.

What Does a Mentoring Session Look Like?

When John Steinbeck set out to write the story of his travel across America with his blue poodle, Charley, he took time to reflect on the nature of a trip. His reflection is a wise place for a mentor to pause:

> A trip, a safari, an exploration, is an entity, different from all other journeys. It has personality, temperament, individuality, uniqueness. A journey is a person in itself; no two are alike. And all plans, safeguards, policing and coercion are fruitless. We find after years of struggle that we do not take a trip; a trip takes us. Tour masters, schedules, reservations, brass-bound and inevitable, dash themselves to wreckage on the personality of the trip.[1]

The same can be said about the process, plan and experience of mentoring: each mentoring relationship too has its own personality, temperament, individuality and uniqueness. The starting place may be a common question or a report on the week, but, "a journey is a person in itself; no two are alike."[2] When the mentor accepts that, an hour of mentoring becomes a travelogue unique unto itself. Steinbeck also lamented the tyranny of maps: "I know people who are so immersed in road maps that they never see the countryside they pass through."[3] I say, let the mentee's journey tell the story and let the mentor start as a passenger who listens well.

Each mentor in my life started the process with their own distinctive approach. Each mentor will have their own practice for how to begin each session. Many create a simple tradition that includes prayer, a check-in and a starting question. Some always start with prayer, verbal or silent. Most have a favorite question to start the conversation and center the work. My best mentors, however, have always seemed to approach our time together as a journey into a new place together.

GLORIA

My first spiritual mentor started at the same place every time we met. She had three questions and repeated them as a framework for our time together—simple words that grounded our work in my story of the most recent past. It didn't mean she didn't take me back to earlier times, but she started with what she considered step one:

1. What was the high moment of the week for you?

2. What was the low moment of the week for you?

3. How faithful were you in keeping the disciplines to which you committed yourself at our last meeting?

TOM

Tom is someone I know to be a deeply skilled and wise spiritual director. He often starts his session with an equally simple question that grounds the conversation in the immediacy of story as well. "What came into the room with you today?" It's actually a brilliant question because it invites the mentee to tell their own story in a way that further invites the mentor to participate in it. Never an empty exercise in going over the calendar of the previous week, step one is an invitation for the mentee to ponder and write their own meaning of the recent past. It grounds the work in life as it has been lived, questions that need to be asked and issues that need to be raised. Always, he begins with prayer.

DAN

Another mentor I know goes to an Old Testament story. Jacob was on the run. He had cheated his brother, lied to his father, abandoned his responsibilities and fled his home. In the Genesis narrative of Jacob it is said he wrestled with a man until daybreak. The man could not prevail against Jacob, but he struck his hip, thus dislocating it and leaving Jacob with a limp. He said to Jacob, "Let me go, for the day is breaking." But Jacob said, "I will not let you go unless you bless me." So he did what God often does with us, "He said to him, 'What is your name?' And he said, 'Jacob.' Then the man said, 'You shall no longer be called Jacob, but Israel, for you have striven with God and with humans, and have prevailed" (Genesis 32:26-28). The name Israel means "one who strives with God." The chosen people of God are those who strive with God. In *The Message*, we read, "Your name is no longer Jacob. From now it's Israel (God-Wrestler); you've wrestled with God, and you've come through" (Genesis 32:28). Dan's mentoring question is: "Where are you striving with God now?" There is often silence, but never have the mentees been stumped.

How would you answer that question even now as you read the words? *Where are you striving with God?* It is not an easy question for us to answer quickly; that's what makes it a good mentoring question. Good questions aren't answered with a simple yes or no. Jacob's experience is universal because there is wrestling within our souls that is common to us all. When I say we learn to read our story, we are learning to name where we strive with God in the living of life.

WILLIAM

On a silent retreat, we started our work by reading a text from the Gospel of John. In John 1 we read that Jesus was doing what he seemed to be doing often: he was walking around. When he walked past two of John's disciples, John declared him to be "the Lamb of God." The two began to follow Jesus, and he turned and asked, "What are you looking for?" (John 1:37-38). It became the persistent, sometimes haunting question for my entire retreat. "What are you looking for?" It is one of our most basic human questions. Each time William and I met he read a Scripture text to me, asked me to listen and left me with a question. I had to make a shift: I was the listener and his question "what are you looking for?" was not easy.

JOHN

For nearly a year John and I met in a suburban office park at least monthly. Our sessions lasted two hours and were never rushed. We came together to explore my ministry and personal growth. He was a pastor with a long history working with leaders facing challenges at the intersection of professional life and spiritual life. Therapist-like, he usually started with a catch-all question about what I'd be thinking about since we last met. "How are things going?" became a portal for me to propose the question, problem, issue or concern I wanted to explore. More directive than others I have known, he often took an active lead and said, "What I'd like us to explore isn't directly what you've asked but, since we have time, let's see where the questions take us." Always we seemed to circle back to integrate my presenting question that day. I don't know how he did it.

It wasn't forced or scripted, but he seemed comfortable with something that was on his mind and even framed from his own experiences as a pastor over forty years of life. He was one I consider an accountability mentor for me. He wanted to explore cracks in my armor, blind spots in my vision and gaps in my decision making. He was direct, bold and insistent in setting out our course of conversation—and he was gentle, patient and wise. He took notes, wrote up verbatims on our work and showed me everything he had written. He provided pastoral care, but not without a mentor's heart and mind. The outcome was to help me listen to God's voice in parts of my life and work where it had been muted. He was the most "authoritative" of any mentor I've had, but one of the most effective. I came to trust him very early because he told me what I didn't always want to hear, and he did so in a humble spirit of love and respect.

JEREMIAH

There are six verbs in Jeremiah 1:10; each verb is a necessary conversation with a mentee at one time or another so I consider Jeremiah a mentor for us. "See, today I appoint you over nations and kingdoms to uproot and tear down, to destroy and overthrow, to build and to plant" (NIV). As a young prophet with a word to speak to his people, culture, and community, Jeremiah was given instructions to engage the people around six different activities needed in his time. Each offers a doorway to the inner sanctuary where the story is being written. Jeremiah's instructions were given to help him read the many ways the story of his people might unfold. There is indirection here when many insist on direct and clear plotlines. There are conflicting and competing actions in the story of Israel that will create dissonance and confusion. Reading the

plotlines of our life stories requires familiarity with multiple plotlines that unfold in life.

To uproot is to pull out the weeds in someone's life by speaking
truth about the damage weeds can do to healthy plants. The mentor
is courageous to speak truth about those activities, images and
viewpoints that are destructive to the mentee and to others. To
uproot is to help prune the branches to give the plant health. It is
not an act of judgment but one of truth telling.

To tear down is to deconstruct false images and worldviews that
limit our receptivity to God. Uprooting is hard work, but tearing
down is disruptive in a caringly confronting way. There are idols,
false images and ideas that mentees can hold as sacred, and at times,
it is the role of the mentor to be part of the deconstructive project
in order to be help rebuild.

To destroy is to create disillusionment for a mentee, something I
believe is ultimately a positive process. We destroy illusions that a
mentee has of their own wisdom or destructiveness, overconfidence
or strength. Mentors must tread carefully in this realm of destruction. After several sessions with one of my mentees, I asked if
she knew herself to be loved by her father. It is a question one of
my mentors asked me once, and it haunted me for years. She told
me she had done some things in her adolescence that disappointed
her family and said she knew that God was equally disappointed in
her. Her illusion of God was a mirror reflection of her father. As
her father's disappointment grew into judgment, she felt God's
judgment on her choices and decisions. "Will you read a verse every
day for the next thirty days?" I asked. "It's not long." The text is
from Paul: "There is therefore now no condemnation for those who
are in Christ Jesus" (Romans 8:1). The impact was not immediate,
but the destruction of her view of an angry, judgmental God who
held her in contempt gave way to the God revealed elsewhere in

Paul: "Do you despise the riches of his kindness and forbearance and patience? Do you not realize that God's kindness is meant to lead you to repentance?" (Romans 2:4). The illusion of contempt slowly was destroyed as a new reality of God's kindness took root in her soul.

To overthrow is to help a person say no to something that is harmful for them, an addiction or habitual choice that keeps them from saying yes to something healthy for them. Mentees are often victims of or simply blocked by addictive or habitual choices that cast a dark shadow on their lives. Mentors need to shine light on such behaviors, choices and ideas. "Have you ever connected your struggle with pornography and your image of God as one who judges?" "Could it be that you have lost your motivation for ministry because you find yourself obsessed by your hope for promotion?" One of the important questions often asked by mentors is "What are you afraid of?" "What keeps you bound and blocked?" Often a mentee knows but hasn't yet named it out loud.

Many of us raised in cultures of guilt and shame are seriously blocked from accepting the good and the noble within. Perhaps that's why Brennan Manning received such an emotional response from many in evangelical settings. He would end every sermon or session by playing some music and inviting the audience to picture themselves being taken into the arms and seated on the lap of Jesus who says, "God has a word intended only for you right now. What is it?" Many are blocked from the words of Yahweh, "I know the plans I have for you, says the LORD, plans for your welfare and not for harm, to give you a future with hope" (Jeremiah 29:11).

To build is to start with a foundation and carefully help a mentee design a spiritual, mental and emotional home—a place of safety and relationship. It might seem the easiest and most natural inclination for mentors, but sometimes it is not. We never tear down and deconstruct except to build. There are moments where, as a mentor, I have felt ready to judge, condemn, reject—to tear down—and have lost sight of the outcome: to build a foundation for a long life of spiritual growth.

> Unless the LORD builds the house,
>   those who build it labor in vain.
> Unless the LORD guards the city,
>   the guard keeps watch in vain. (Psalm 127:1)

To plant is to put good seeds into receptive soil for germination and growth. The challenge for new mentors is to have patience enough to wait for germination to prompt the eventual growth that a mentor may wish was present today rather than in "due time." One of Thomas Merton's most important books is called *New Seeds of Contemplation*.[4] His simple premise that every moment has the possibility of planting seeds in us has nurtured people all over the world. Our vocation in life is to work together with God to receive the good seeds so they are planted in the good soil of our own inner landscape. But Merton won't leave it there; he continues the beautiful metaphor. Not only are there seeds to be received, he says, but "God utters me like a word containing a partial thought of Himself. A word will never be able to comprehend the voice that utters it."[5] In addition to being receptors of God, we are the very word God speaks. My life, identity and purpose are a word spoken distinctively by God into the world. "But, if I am true to the concept that God utters in me, if I am true to the thought of Him I was meant to embody, I shall be full of His actuality and find Him everywhere in myself and find myself nowhere. I shall be lost in Him: that is I shall find myself. I shall be 'saved.'"[6]

MENTORING AS MORE THAN THERAPY

I've said from page one that spiritual mentoring is a reflective, almost contemplative experience. We listen and read the story of the mentee. The imagery we choose is important for our understanding of the role. Am I a counselor, evangelist, judge, teacher, tutor, coach, personal life trainer or priest? Am I friend, host, companion, guide or fellow traveler? In the past years my practice has shifted toward the latter list. I have come to believe that we join the mentee in their story and, in time, become part of the story with them. The temptation is for mentoring to become an inexpensive form of therapy as I sit in the presence of a professional spiritual listener who is better trained than me to know God. I'm not sure that's how Jesus prepared his disciples. He prepared them not for professional ministry but for profound spiritual friendship. He taught them to listen, see, follow, wait, pray, enter, engage, encounter, break bread, sit at table and be present.

THE CURRICULUM OF MENTORING

Spiritual mentoring is learning to read at least three things: Torah (Scripture), *telos* (purpose) and *kairos* (timeliness).

Torah is a Hebrew word for law or guidance by the mind and heart of God. It refers not only to biblical teachings, as essential and foundational as they are, but also to guidance by Spirit of spirit. Torah was the scripture for Jesus; it is textual—in his world it was contained in scrolls and included the Pentateuch, the first five books of the Bible. "And I will walk among you, and will be your God, and you shall be my people" (Leviticus 26:12). But Torah in ancient Israel was more than written text. In the rabbinic tradition there was an oral component that had its source in the encounter with Moses on Mount Sinai. We tend to forget this part in the Christian church. The Torah contained two parts: the *Torah*

Shebichtav, which means "Torah that is written," and *Torah Shebe'al Peh*, which means "Torah that is spoken." Found in Talmud (the collection of rabbinic understandings of Law) and Midrash (sermons, exegesis of the Law), Torah is handed to the next generation. In Luke we have a literal experience of this when "the scroll of the prophet Isaiah was given to him [Jesus]" (Luke 4:17), and he began to interpret its meaning. The synagogue community figuratively and literally held the text and gave it to Jesus, who told them what it meant. In Greek there is a word, *paralambano*, used by the apostle Paul to describe the tradition as it was passed forward: "We also constantly give thanks to God for this, that when you received [*paralambano*] the word of God that you heard from us, you accepted it not as a human word but as what it really is, God's word, which is also at work in you believers" (1 Thessalonians 2:13).

Likewise, the mentoring experience is a *paralambano* experience: we listen, as did Jesus, to the living voice, and we wrestle to know the meaning of the written Word. Most likely, this is not a Bible study with the mentee as much as an opportunity to read and listen to selected texts in the context of the mentee's story. We were created for this kind of "textual intimacy." The text doesn't just *contain* the voice of God as the Declaration of Independence *contains* the voice of its writers; it is the continuously living voice of God, which we have mute in our churches when we treat it as an ancient library text or script for a previous generation. The exegetical work needed today starts with belief that God still has something to say and that Scripture is one of God's best ways to for us to continue our conversation with God. Our journey to holiness or spiritual maturity takes us through biblical text. It's not just interesting and outdated letters, law, history and poetry, it is the voice of God handed forward in living form. It was through Torah that an entire culture came to know who they were, and each person in that culture knew themselves as a distinctive part. Created in the image of God, we are each part of God's story. It has been said in poetic beauty that each person is a letter in the alphabet that together makes up humankind. We are uniquely ourselves as an *a* or *k* or *w*, but we need the rest of the alphabet to tell a story. As we live in relationship with each other, we learn to read the vocabulary of the soul in the voice of Torah.

Telos is a Greek word that means purpose or outcome, the end game colloquially. We read the life story of mentees alertly, listening for purpose. Jesus' *telos* became known to him over his lifetime until he could say, "I have come to seek and to save the lost," but let us be clear: that was Jesus' *telos*; yours and mine must also be discerned over time. We may call this vocational discernment or discovering one's calling. For some it may be choosing their career; for all who follow Jesus discernment is our way of living with the conviction of *telos*. We live aware that our life has intention—it's something given to us, not merely chosen. If there is no God, there is no coherence to my story—it's only a series of random events, and I can choose to be and do anything I please. If there is no God, there is no intentionality to life at all. The only accountability is to myself. I may choose altruism or narcissism, a photo album of selfies or of others, but in the end, there is merely fate. The way of Torah leads us to *telos*— a way of life in God believing, in faith, there is coherence in the apparent randomness of life. In a conversation with a friend yesterday he professed his certainty: "I am here in this job at this time in my life because God wants me here." In mentoring we pay attention to *telos*. Interestingly enough, the word *teleios* in Greek has been translated "perfect" as a call to spiritual completeness or maturity.

Kairos is a Greek word that grounds the unseen in your story. *Kairos* means the opportune moment, the ripe or even timely time. Paul said, "In the fullness of time, God sent Jesus." In time. Time is also a deeply spiritual reality. We cannot see it, but we live in it like a fish lives in water. Spirituality is paying attention to meaning in time—to those things that make certain moments timely. If there is no God, time is only made up of disconnected moments that follow each other without direction, meaning or purpose. Attention to *kairos* is attention to what some call "locatedness" in particular moments of history and story. It grounds story in the locatedness of here and now. Without demeaning past or future, *kairos* says with emphasis, "Wake up, pay attention, look around, notice, become aware, listen and know!" Monastics in the Benedictine tradition were given one word from their leader, Benedict of Nursia, in fourth-century Italy: *listen*. Listening is the way we are present to time, to self, to another, to God. Listening is not something you can do in retrospect—it is not remembering; listening is the way we attend to here and now in the fullness of time. That means we listen *in* the present moment attentive to the revelation in all things ordinary, but it also means we listen *for* the present moment. To what am I called *here and now*? Oddly enough, most of my mentees who came wanting to talk about "spirituality" ended up talking about jobs, family, heartbreak, crises and pain. And those who said they wanted to talk about jobs, family, heartbreak, crises and pain ended up talking about where God is found in the midst of those things.

If there is a curriculum for mentoring it will include attention to Torah, *telos* and *kairos*.

- We learn to listen as God guides our way of life, so we ask, "What is God breathing into my life through Scripture, worship, meditation, silence, contemplation, readings, retreats and any of the myriad ways God's Spirit uses to guide us in the way?" "Who am I as I learn Torah, the way of life in God?" One of my favorite questions is "What are you reading in scripture that causes you to say, 'Huh?'" Not a sophisticated method but an effective one. As we tune our ears to listen and our eyes to read Torah as the living word of God, we begin to see and hear. It is a discipline practiced every day by ordinary people committed to daily encounter with the living God. What do I hear as I discipline myself to pay attention? From the field of neuroscience we learn, "Biologically speaking, there is no off switch for attention in the brain. Rather, our attention is trained in one direction or another. . . . We're always paying attention to something."[7] We learn to discern the purpose of our life, giftedness, agency and capacity, so we ask, "What's next for my faithfulness in the stewardship of all I've been given?

- We learn to imagine the purpose of our life, giftedness, agency and capacity so we ask, "What's next for my faithfulness in the stewardship of all I've been given, and what is the purpose that leads me to care for the poor, the widows and orphans, and to seek healing redemption for people and systems within my circle of influence?"

- We learn to read the time in which we live and the meaning that makes it timely, so we ask, "Where is God active in our history, culture, neighborhoods and world, and what is God writing in the moments of my own story and our story as a couple, family or household? Is there a new direction for my family me? Do I sense a movement from God for what's next in my life?" We each have a circle of influence, people and systems we are able to assist, guide and maybe even change. What does God desire for your circle of influence?

This is spirituality. You should recognize it as your life. You should recognize the questions as questions we each ask in our own way: Who am I? What's next? Where is God active right now?

We are never far from text and voice in mentoring. At least, we should not be far from scriptural text in spiritual mentoring. There is temptation to be seduced by the sound of our own wisdom as mentors. There is the lure of making the periphery into the center. Spiritual mentoring, as I envision it, is grounded in Torah. We are listening in all the ways people of faith have listened to God speak, but especially through Scripture. The Rule of Benedict is wise: "Let us set out on the way with the Gospel as our guide."[8] Early spiritual directors knew to follow the lead of St. Benedict. How they proceeded was not prescribed, but it is fair to say that Christian spiritual mentoring has always been a bridge to Scripture. The Bible is not a resource like an FAQ section on a website; reading Scripture is one way we ground our entire life in God.

THE ROLE OF SCRIPTURE IN MENTORING

Central to Christian faith is immersion and consistent dialogue with God *in Scripture*. That is the grounding for mentoring. I'm not talking about a romantic kind of philosophical discourse or sentimentality. The early Christian writers were schooled not only in prayer but in the Psalms, Gospels and all biblical texts. They brought their personal experience to spiritual direction, but they were also grounded in biblical understanding. They shared their wisdom with their mentees and interpreted the mentee's life through Scripture. They were unafraid to use biblical imagery, vocabulary and texts, and the scriptures were central to their work. For classical Christian spiritual directors, Scripture was always in the room, on the table and part of the conversation. Many of them lived, as we increasingly do, in a contested space. How did they persist in places and times of embattled faith? I am drawn to an image in Nehemiah 8 for my answer. Israel is on the way back to Jerusalem after years in exile in Babylon. As the people settled into their new homes and were restored to the land they had lost decades earlier, Ezra, the scholar-priest, did something unusual, unexpected and perhaps unprecedented in their experience: he climbed a tower and read Torah to them from early morning until midday, and the people, gathered in the square, listened. A remarkable scene. "So they read from the book, from the law of God, with interpretation. They gave the sense, so that the people understood the reading" (Nehemiah 8:8). They read and interpreted Scripture because they believed it was truly God's Word given to Israel. Ezra's revolution wasn't political or social; rather, it was textual. He read the Bible to them, grounding them in Torah because he believed it would shape them as a people of faith. And then he led them in worship. His conviction was made public: wisdom is found not only in the human voice but in the Word of God. Wisdom is not only in the instincts, intuition and information given by Ezra the scholar-priest, but in the words of Torah read and interpreted with the people.

How is Scripture used in the mentoring session? In two ways, both of which are important. First, it is present in the room. By that I mean there is an awareness that our conversation is not devoid of our biblical context—the living tradition handed forward. It is present in the mind of the mentor and in the conversations. I'm not talking about finding a biblical "sermonette" for every experience of the mentee but rather about speaking with the integrity of those biblical people whose lives and faith are revelatory. Second, it may serve as a starting place, stopping place or ending place. I often begin a mentoring session by reading a biblical text aloud. I may stop in the middle of the session to recite or read a text apropos the conversation. I often end the session with a Scripture as prayer, benediction or assignment. My Bible always sits on my desk. It is not part of the piles of work that may clutter my desk; it is there, always at hand, as is my CIA coffee mug, waiting to be used and offering nourishment (I think coffee has nutrients). Just as the empty chair is a symbol for the presence of the Spirit, so the Bible is a symbol for the speaking voice of Torah.

What mentoring does *not* promise is answers, solutions, resolution, affirmation, reformation, formation or guidance; rather, what mentoring will give is more questions, problems, issues, confrontation, deformation, disillusionment and new terrain that will require a new map. Mentoring is listening together to what will be heard. Mentoring becomes ineffective when it replaces presence with answers and solutions. We are in the business of helping people learn how to read. I don't believe I can say that often or loudly enough.

Asking Great Questions

I hope you know someone who understands the power of the interrogative. My friend Dave is someone in my life who asks questions, the kind that won't let you go. His are not questions to be answered by a simple yes or no, up or down, chicken or beef. They draw you into a deep place. Mentoring is the craft of asking great questions. I have been asked great questions in my life. Over the years I have collected my own list of what I consider some of the best questions I have been asked or heard. I offer it as a resource guide for mentors in the ongoing work of mentoring. It is a starting place for learning to ask good questions.

1. *What's chasing you?* I had just emailed a man I considered a mentor and told him about a busy and successful season of teaching, speaking, writing and traveling. Rather than receiving an "Atta boy" shout out from him, his email asked one stark question: "What's chasing you?" He heard my busyness as a sign of escape from myself and from God.

2. *Are you at peace?* I first heard this question and learned it as a common tribal greeting in certain African cultures. Swap it out for the common greeting "How's it going?" and see how the

question itself requires you to slow down and tell the story of your recent days to answer it. You cannot answer this question without telling your story.

3. *When you were ten, did you feel yourself to be loved by your father?* In the middle of a phone call with a mentor we were talking about a book project he was working on when he ambushed me with this question. It took me completely by surprise, and I finally stuttered, "No, I don't think so. I know he loved me because I was one of his children, but it was not something I felt." My mentor's response was, "I quite thought it was that." He didn't return to the question immediately, but it was a topic of conversation for us again.

4. *What would you do with your life "for free" if you didn't need any income?* I suppose no question stirs the search for vocational clarity as does this one.

5. *Do you know anyone who lives the kind of spirituality you put on yourself?* In a mentoring session I found myself distracted by a mentee whose words were an echo of my own inner storyteller's words of shame about perfection, performance and production. It wasn't so much that I asked him the question as that I knew the question was for me. I know that spirituality is often code language for guilt, judgment and shame.

6. *When was the last time you remember being content?* Profound.

7. *Why do you always "should" on yourself?* This came from Brennan, who said his mentor had those words engraved on a plaque on her desk so she could see them each day. I am an expert at this. I know how to "should" on myself and probably fall prey to it every day.

8. *What do you know that, had you known it twenty-five years ago, would have made a difference in your life these past twenty-five*

years? I was hosting a man who would later become an occasional mentor in my life. He was exactly twenty-five years older than I was, and this question popped into my head as we stood in a cafeteria line. His answers were swift: "I now know you can't get back time you've lost with your family" was first. Then he said, "I didn't know then that the most important things in my life would happen when I was not in control, and I've spent most of the last twenty-five years trying to get in control."

9. *When have you known yourself to be loved, celebrated and delighted in?* Enough said.

10. *As you look back over the past decade, is there anything you wish you could get back? How does that inform your next decade?* It sounds like a question a broker might ask, but it's a question that invites a "long enough" reflection on one's story.

11. *If you were to create a "to-don't" list to place alongside your to-do list, what are three things you would write first?* I don't know where it came from, but it's valuable to remember that *no* is a complete sentence.

12. *"Our gifts and our wounds are one." These words were given to me by a mentee. What is the grief you still carry? And what is the grief you still need to embrace as gift?* If grief is our common human experience, we don't get to evade this one.

13. *In what ways, specifically, have you become intolerant of mystery?*

14. *Why do you persist?* A colleague gave me a copy of John Terpstra's book *Skin Boat: Acts of Faith and Other Navigations.* In it he writes, "I have asked myself, *why do I persist?*"[1] That is the question of the entire book. It is a profound way to ask, "Why am I still an apprentice of Jesus? After all that I now know of others and myself and the world, why do I persist in faith?"[2]

15. *What are the questions that have captivated, haunted or motivated you?* The questions that drive us, compel, captivate and haunt us are as important as the answers we find.

16. *To measure your success in your profession, look into the face of your spouse. What story does it tell?* I don't know where this question came from, but I know that it has told me of my own failure as a husband and also my joy in my wife's forgiveness and love.

17. *If Jesus invited you to climb into his lap and whispered something in your ear, what would he say to you about yourself right now?* I remember the first time I heard Brennan Manning ask that question in Philadelphia. I was riveted by the question because I struggled to know how I might answer the question. He repeated the question every time I heard him speak.

Wisdom for
the Long Walk of Faith

I met Henri Nouwen when I was a young pastor in Tacoma, Washington. My memory of the day is vivid. I was part of a community organization that brought him to our city for a peacemaking conference in the early 1980s. His plane arrived late into SeaTac airport because of a common problem in our state: fog. Henri walked onto the stage, and I remember that he pulled off his sweatshirt over his head in a way that left strands of hair loose in the wind. He never noticed. He was introduced, started to speak, and two hours later finished an afternoon of riveting teaching I will never forget. He didn't use a single note or text. It flowed from his mind, heart and soul. I prayed with him before a lunch after the conference and was privileged to stand beside him and to have my hand grasped by his as we stood in a prayer circle in a south Tacoma neighborhood.

I remember September 21, 1996, just as vividly. I sat in my third-floor office looking out on the Kresge Courtyard on the Bethel College campus when the news came. Henri had died. The tears were involuntary and the grief immediate. I had read every book he had written and counted him a spiritual teacher, though our contacts were limited. His writing captured the voice with the Dutch accent I first heard at Pacific Lutheran University that day in Tacoma. My sadness in his passing was that his voice would no longer be available in his words. I was wrong. The Henri J. M. Nouwen Estate has done a masterful job since his death in recrafting his work in new books based on his earlier teaching. One of the best speaks with his voice: *Spiritual Direction: Wisdom for the Long Walk of Faith.*

The book contains these words of Nouwen's: "Spiritual direction [mentoring] provides an 'address' on the house of your life so you can be 'addressed' by God in prayer."[1] Those words etch the purpose and process of spiritual guidance on the mind of anyone receptive to them. Nouwen was a priest and undoubtedly practiced spiritual formation in a formal protocol, but he also lived his life outside of the priestly role as spiritual friend to mentally disabled adults for whom spiritual direction would make little sense. What makes profound sense is what his words evoke for me in the experience I have every time I sit with a receptive mentee seeking to know themselves, God and their story. Nouwen understood the spiritual life as "a long walk of faith," not simply a collection of short steps, missteps, meanderings or detours. While detours may be a common experience of spiritual life, we're most importantly on the "long walk of faith" as we listen to the active voice of God as we are addressed by him. I love Henri's words because they evoke awareness of a constantly unfolding story. Spiritual mentoring is an invitation to listen to the unfolding of a large story as *God addresses you* as you learn to listen deeply. My name is on the envelope, scroll and story. It is not dedicated to me as a third-person text; it is addressed to me in the first person and to us as a community in the first person. Listen.

"The first and most essential spiritual practice that any spiritual director [mentor] must ask anyone to pursue is the discipline of the Heart. Introspective and contemplative prayer is the ancient discipline by which we begin to see God in our heart."[2] For centuries spiritual teachers have taught us this method of listening in prayer. "In prayer, we awaken ourselves to God within us. With practice we allow God to enter into our heartbeat, and our breathing, into our thoughts, emotions, into our hearing, seeing, thinking, and tasting, and into every membrane of our body. It is by being awakened to God in us that we can increasingly see God in the world around us."[3]

I periodically teach a course called "Introduction to Spiritual Direction/Spiritual Mentoring." On day one of the class I tell them the truth that spiritual mentoring is about learning to listen to the already active presence of God. I tell them it is learning to listen in prayer. I tell them it is learning to read life as story with the help of another. I tell them that anyone can do it. And then I usually say, "That's it—that's the whole course. We can go home." That's the truth. Spiritual mentoring is sitting with another person in the presence of the Holy Spirit to help them read their life. It requires capacities that are common to all followers of Jesus:

- Ears to hear and eyes to see
- Spiritual curiosity
- Wisdom to share
- Humility of heart and honesty of life

THE SCIENCE AND ART OF MENTORING

Why then does my course last an additional fifteen hours, and why is this book longer than one chapter? Because spiritual mentoring, while not a professional skill, requires focus and wisdom. There is both science and art in the craft of mentoring. We may be adept at watching a movie or reading a novel but need help to prayerfully read our own lives as story. It seems we have lost something about story along the way. Perhaps what has been lost is the communal fire where whole villages gathered to tell stories to each other and to teach the young about stories. Perhaps what has been lost is the village green where whole communities gathered to sell goods, share the news, gossip and tell stories to each other. And definitely what is missing in our culture is the role of the mentor and apprentice: where mothers sat with daughters to teach household economics and skills and to give wisdom about life; where fathers taught sons mostly how to do the work of farming, carpentry, finance and business and to share wisdom about life; and where grandparents sat around a family table to tell stories of life and children learned from each of the generations present. Because our culture is thin in those experiences, we need help learning how to do this kind of listening and reading.

Spiritual mentoring is methodical in the way that storytelling has a foundational structure of plot, character development and dialogue, but it is not formulaic. More like the "choose your own adventure" style of children's books, mentoring invites us into a space of discerning the next question, taking the next turn and listening deeply for the next pause. Mentoring is a subset of disciple making, I suppose, as disciple making is a subset of spiritual formation. But spiritual mentoring starts with story and follows the path of relational curiosity. I recently asked Tom, one of the gifted mentors I know and a spiritual director in the Anglican tradition, to conduct a mentoring session in front of a class of students. He was not self-conscious as he began. He started with a short description of his "technique": "I let them know I am not in a hurry. I tell them we will listen together, and I invite them to become very present to what is emerging in themselves. And then I pray for them." When we rush or feel rushed we are motivated to find answers, solutions, the quick fix, the resolution or closure. Spirituality is about wisdom for the long walk of faith.

NEURAL PATHWAYS OF GROWTH

It matters that you can sit in something slow and focus on the long walk of faith. The world of neuroscience is on to something we need to know. William James, in his 1890 book *The Principles of Psychology*, has this terrifying quote: "In most of us, by the age of thirty, the character has set like plaster, and will never soften again."[4] But wait, I'm not sure I liked who I was as a thirty-year-old pastor, husband and father of three. Tell me today's neuroscience has better news for me than that! Are we actually "set in stone" by thirty, unable to grow? Deborah Ancona gives us the news, "It turns out that we, as human beings, develop neural pathways, and the more we use those neural pathways over years and years and years, they become very stuck and deeply embedded, moving into deeper portions of the brain."[5] But there is hope. Tara Swart, a senior lecturer at MIT, talks about it in her book *Neuroscience for Leadership*. Ancona and Swart have identified three steps required to create new connections between neurons. They might sound familiar.

Focused attention. "This is the only way you'll actually grow new neurons strong enough to connect with existing neurons, forming new pathways."[6] By focused attention she means any "energy intensive" challenge that requires "conscious processing of inputs, conscious decision making, complex problem solving, memorizing complex concepts, planning, strategizing, self-reflection, regulating our emotions and channeling energy from them, exercising self-control and willpower."[7] I nearly fell off my chair when I read those words. Without exaggeration, this is the slow work we're describing in this book. Learning to pay attention not only brings spiritual growth but it changes neural pathways! Jesus was more simple and direct: "But blessed are your eyes, for they see, and your ears, for they hear" (Matthew 13:16).

Deliberate repetition and practice. "Depending on the complexity of the activity, (experiments have required) four and a half months, 144 days or even three months for a new brain map, equal in complexity to an old one, to be created in the motor cortex."[8] She adds, "During this time, motivation, willpower and self-control are necessary to achieve your goal."[9] Ancient spirituality has practiced this for centuries—we call it liturgy, daily prayer, weekly Sabbath, regular pilgrimage and sacred reading. It includes the daily examen and contemplative prayer Nouwen taught us. It is what Brother Lawrence simplified centuries ago: practicing the presence of God in the kitchen, on the job and in everything you do.

The right environment. Our brain's need to survive keeps us focused on the sources of danger, threat, escape and battle. The right environment for developing new neural connections, however, is a place that creates an environment of creativity, relationship and innovation. You need hydration, nutrients and rest "as your brain learns, unlearns, and relearns behavioral patterns."[10] Mentoring is that "right environment" for growth as we listen.

Focused attention, deliberate repetition and practice, and the right environment. Spiritual writers across the centuries would simply nod and say, "Yes, of course, that's the way spirituality is formed in people. That is wisdom for the long walk of faith."

LISTENING TO THE EVERYDAY

We don't grow and mature in our Christian life by sitting in a classroom and library, listening to lectures and reading books or going to church and singing hymns and listening to sermons. We do it by taking the stuff of our ordinary lives, our parents and children, our spouses and friends, our work-places and fellow workers, our dreams and fantasies, our at-tachments, our easily accessible gratifications, our deperson-alizing of intimate relations, our commodification of living truths into idolatries, taking all this and placing it on the altar of refining fire—our God is a consuming fire—and finding it all stuff redeemed for a life of holiness.[11]

I look for others to help me learn to read the stuff of our or-dinary lives. I learned spirituality as something separate from my relationships, family life, work life, physical needs, financial values or social context. I've needed help to listen in the most ordinary moments of life. It is often the poets, writers and songwriters who help me the most.

Try this out. Listen to the song "Holy as a Day Is Spent" on your phone or on iTunes, or read the words with a curious mind. The songwriter and singer is Carrie Newcomer. Her poetry and music is often gritty and filled with wonder about the most everyday things.[12]

Holy as a day is spent
holy is the dish and drain
the soap and sink, and the cup and plate
and the warm wool socks, and the cold white tile
showerheads and good dry towels
and frying eggs sound like psalms
with bits of salt measured in my palm
it's all a part of a sacrament
as holy as a day is spent
Holy is the busy street

and cars that boom with passion's beat
and the checkout girl, counting change
and the hands that shook my hands today
and hymns of geese fly overhead
and spread their wings like their parents did
blessed be the dog that runs in her sleep
to chase some wild and elusive thing

Newcomer understands spirituality as a natural part of life, with "speech" taking on the forms of dish towels, geese, dogs, cars and wool socks. She seems to believe the world is alive with the many voices of God; her music sees with eyes of faith. Spirituality is daily disciplined curiosity, which is another phrase for reflective listening because it is curiosity about

- the ordinary

- our own story

- the story of the other in relationships

- *the* story in the gospel

- our story in community

- the mystery of the presence of the living God in the moments of our life

- what can be seen in the most ordinary things and heard in the most common sounds

HOLY CURIOSITY

Music is one of the best teachers for learning to read languages of soul because songs are so often *in vivo*, about the living of life. Why would it be otherwise? Frederick Buechner speaks of life itself as sacrament. "A sacrament is when something holy happens. It is transparent time, time which you can see through to something deep inside time. . . . If we weren't as blind as bats, we might see that life itself is sacramental."[13] Learning the language of faith starts with paying attention in holy curiosity.

I have never met a child who is not curious. I am privileged to know seven children who call me by various names for grandpa: two call me Bumpa, two call me Papa and three call me Baba. When they are teenagers, I expect they'll struggle to find a name to use in public; I suspect it will become grandpa. These seven are a living ecosystem of curiosity. All love Legos and build what their imagination proposes. Some love to dance and sing original, never-before-performed renditions of music that soars from their own spirits, bodies and souls. Some love numbers, others history or science, and all are captivated by animations of story. The energy of their curiosity is a thing of beauty. They are each endlessly curious. They are learning to read the universe.

The opposite of curiosity, I suppose, is closed-mindedness and a sense of boring, predictable banality. "I've been there before," "I've already seen, felt, tasted, touched, heard or done that before." *Disinterest* is a common antonym for curiosity; *normality* is another. To be frozen in "the normal" instead of open to surprise is a form of disinterest. Jesus said repeatedly, "Look, the kingdom of God is over there, do you see it?" It is the sine qua non of the mentor—in fresh ways we ask Jesus' question again and again, "Look the kingdom of God is here, now; it is there in memory and story. Look, it is over there, do you see it?" Curiosity breeds curiosity. Mentor curiosity becomes mentee curiosity.

Scripture tells the story of Moses at work one day. He was a shepherd at that time, hiding out from Egyptian authorities. On this particular day he saw something he had seen many times before, I suspect: a bush on fire in the desert. In an arid setting, a bit of sand set free by the wind can ignite a dry bush and spark it into flames. For some reason, on this day, Moses stopped what he was doing. "He looked, and the bush was blazing, yet it was not consumed" (Exodus 3:2). So he did a logical thing that turned out to be a sacramental thing. "Moses said, 'I must turn aside and look at this great sight, and see why the bush is not burned up'" (Exodus 3:3). The words "Sabbath" and "sabbatical" are rooted in a Hebrew word that means simply, sometimes painfully, stop. Stop and turn aside. Stop and look. Stop long enough to see, long enough for focused attention. It became, for Moses, a sacrament in which God spoke the words of dazzling beauty: "Come no closer! Remove the sandals from your feet, for the place on which you are standing is holy ground" (Exodus 3:5).

SLOW WALKING ON HOLY GROUND

For several years I commuted by riding a bicycle to my office. It's a Seattle kind of thing—from home to the ferry to downtown and then to my office. After a shoulder surgery I made the move from wheels to feet. I now walk about two and a half miles every day to get to and from my office. Walking changed things. It changed me. Walking is slower than riding, slower than driving. Walking is different than being driven. Spirituality, I daresay, is walking together in story. Anyone who spends time in the gospel knows that Jesus walked—everywhere. It was a primary mode of transportation in his day, but what if there's more to it than it? What if it tells us something he wanted to teach us about spirituality? I know there was no bus to Jerusalem or cab to Bethlehem, but I'm captivated by the idea that Jesus, as teacher, has something for us to learn from his active life of walking. I once took a course on the Gospel of Mark that required an atlas of first-century Palestine. More than the other Gospel writers, John Mark studied Jesus' movement from place to place and used an almost formulaic repetition of words that emphasize his going, returning, departing, leaving, crossing, setting out, being led up, coming down, making his way and coming. Mark insists on the reader placing Jesus in the context of place and in the activity of travel, mostly by walking.

What happens when you walk instead of ride or drive?

- It slows you down—that's how you are changed by walking.

- Because you go slower, you can see and hear more. Walking gives you access to fewer places, but you can see and hear more because of speed and proximity. Things and people present themselves to you or you intrude into their space as you walk through the city, village or forest. It's harder to ignore what's right in front of you or across the street or nearby. You're also grounded in a literal sense, and that changes you too. What you can see and hear is limited by the scope of pedestrian travel. It also increases your attention to what is now literally right before you or nearby.

- Often you can't avoid encounters with people. In fact, walking creates encounters with people. In Seattle we tend to walk "past" people more than in the Midwest where I once lived, but even here you bump into people, intentionally or not.

- You are more vulnerable when you are on foot. It makes you more accessible. It makes it more possible for opportunity and danger to confront you with surprise. A burning bush that you might miss when driving in a car becomes an encounter you cannot ignore.

- Walking also means you're not running. We run away *from* and we run *toward*. Of course, we can walk *past* other people, but the instinct to run or escape is different than walking.

- Walking means you're not driving or being driven. Being driven describes the busyness of most people I know. Most can quickly show me or describe a calendar that is full or overfull. Fewer can show scheduled times for rest and generative space. I once made an agreement with my colleague Jim that we would call each other out when we heard the other overemphasize the speed of our lives. It usually takes help to practice the long, slow walk of faith.

- When you walk in my city it's harder to ignore homeless people sleeping under the viaduct or near the bridges. I've seen fights break out, drugs being bought and sold, people in tears, accidents occur, and people robbed. And I've seen families laugh, children run, jump and twirl, couples stop to hug and kiss, and moments of loud, unbridled enjoyment.

When people walk *together* more things happen. There is an increased likelihood for humor, verbal intimacy and story. People gesture, point, pause, look and are surprised by interruptions of animals, traffic and other people. I was surprised on a recent walk to see a hillside alive with moving white creatures. It was the lawn-mowing mountain goats that are brought in to eat up the grass on especially steep hillsides in the city. No longer indistinguishable white shapes on a green hilly background, these were actual mountain goats literally chewing up the hillside in downtown Seattle. The cars above and below never saw them.

Mentoring is walking together in spirituality so, I claim, mentoring is slow walking in story. Like my commute in the mornings, you see and look *as you go,* you become vulnerable and subject to interruptions and surprise, you point and pause and stop. Slow walking isn't mindless or purposeless walking; it is, instead, a pace that allows for good conversation. One of my mountain climbing tutors was Ethel McKee. She was then in her seventies and had summited Mount Rainier several times and hiked the Cascades and Olympic mountains for decades. "Walk so that you can easily keep up good conversation." That was her method. "Don't walk so fast you get out of breath and lose the easy pace of conversation. And, she added, "Learn to zigzag back and forth, especially as you walk downhill. It's easier on your knees."

I walk fast most of the time. Spirituality is a slow pace. Slow walking is one of my spiritual disciplines. I'm getting better at it—some days.

Spiritual Mentoring as Ecology

Oikos is the ancient Greek word for household or house. Other meanings of the word include dwelling place, to inhabit, to settle, to live, to belong as a member of the household. *Oikos Theou* refers to the house of God. The English prefix eco-, which moves us into ecology and economics, stems from the word oikos. Oikos is about stewardship or care of the household. Oikos spirituality is the spirituality of all parts of our life in the household of God.

What is the household of God? Or, to put it more bluntly, what matters to God? This is one of the profound questions that needs to be answered by every mentor. Even the language of "spiritual" mentoring implies a limited focus. But the writer of Psalm 24 would have us think in larger, more capacious terms.

> The earth is the Lord's and all that is in it,
> > the world, and those who live in it;
> for he has founded it on the seas,
> > and established it on the rivers. (Psalm 24:1-2)

God's house includes the earth and "all that is in it, the world, and those who live in it" says the poet in Psalm 24. The house of God is not only a sanctuary but what has been suggestively called "an altar in the world."[1] The concerns on God's heart and mind are more than the condition of our soul; they are the larger ecology of "all of life."

Therefore, mentors might craft questions that help mentees consider what God is saying to them about stewardship of all parts of their lives. In an ecosystem, there is health only when the relationships to the various parts of the system are in harmony. It's not hard to see how mighty King David, the man "after God's own heart," may have been a poet and writer of spirituality in his many psalms but needed to spend more time caring for his marriage and children. Prayer is important, yes, but also questions about work, family, relationships, health, pain and the distractions that seem to control life.

All of life is worthy of curiosity for mentors and mentees. The qualifying word, spiritual, does not reduce mentoring as I envision it to prayer or religious practices alone. God's household includes all of the earth, all of life, all of the compartments I inhabit: family, finance, intellect, community, neighborhood, vocation, the culture, the earth, and the world. What is not available material for spiritual mentoring? Abraham Kuyper's statement is rightfully well known. "There is not a square inch in the whole domain of our human existence over which Christ, who is Sovereign over all, does not cry, Mine!"[2]

Creating the Pace

Some of us are very good at starting things. We love the excitement of innovation, the thrill of doing something new, the promise of starting all over. I have spent much of my life in higher education where starting over happens as frequently as every quarter or semester, every year as a new class of first-year students invades the university or graduate school. Starting well takes one kind of skill: setting boundaries, creating vision, developing covenant and inviting trust; sustaining well takes another kind of skill.

We've started well. We meet regularly. Now, how does the mentoring experience "sustain well" over time? Good question.

To sustain well is about setting a pace. Mentor and mentee learn how to work together in the singular uniqueness of their relationship. They meet regularly and continue in the process, but the hope is to continue moving *forward*. There is movement, conversations are animated, anticipation precedes the session and expectations are energized. Some of my colleagues like to talk about learning to "play" together. It's a good image to replace the idea of work because it evokes creativity, energy, fun and storytelling enjoyment. An old Jewish saying asks, "Why were human beings created?" "Because God loves stories."[1]

How does the mentor create a playful pace? As I write this chapter, I am aware that answering that question is a bit like asking someone to define friendship. How do friendships develop from a beginning to something that is perhaps lifelong? Well, it requires trust, continued connection, time, play and more. Friendships aren't based on a series of principles or a sequence of repeated events. Relationships unfold. There aren't seven steps to a successful friendship; there aren't seven steps to sustaining momentum in mentoring, but there are skills to be practiced by both mentor and mentee. It requires *planning on the mentor's part* to nurture relationships and *openness on the mentees part* to bring a consistently teachable spirit. It's not complicated, but it takes work. Spiritual mentoring is relational work. It doesn't require a particular degree, certification or formal education, although each of these may be helpful. It doesn't demand ordination, gray hair or formal theological education. Mentoring requires something more challenging such as listening ears, relational trust, and responsive engagement.

LISTENING EARS

Mentoring requires good questions, but something more is needed: listening ears. Picture a room with three chairs. In one chair sits the mentor, comfortably relaxed as he or she asks good questions. Across from the mentor sits the mentee engaged in animated, thoughtful and reflective response. The third chair is empty, or appears that way to the human eye. That chair is symbolic of the living presence of the Holy Spirit. No one said it with such poetic economy as Aelred of Rivaulx: "Here we are, you and I, and I hope a third, Christ, is in our midst."[2] To whom does the mentor listen? To whom does the mentee give attention? To each other and to the speaking voice of the Spirit. I often set a chair in a place visible to me in the room as a physical reminder of God's presence.

The role of the mentor is to nurture the relationship through good hospitality. The mentor knows how to create a structure and comfortable space for receptive listening ears. It is like the work of the gardener to prepare the soil:

- To create a space welcoming the mentee to be safe and open.

- To create a space with boundaries of confidentiality, structure and guidance.

- To create a space that fosters ideas, curiosity, wonder and joy.

- To create a space that honors the mundane as containers of holy grace.

- To create a space in which the mentee finds freedom to be honest, vulnerable and self-disclosing.

- To create a space in which both are able to walk slowly enough in the story of the mentee to read deeply and well.

- To create a listening space where both will actively wait on the Spirit of the Lord for insight and wisdom. Good mentors are never afraid of empty spaces, which are often better called a time for "the holy pause" in which both allow the silence to be filled by God's spirit who may give a gentle nudge, a whisper or a thunderous roar. I have experienced all of these in mentoring sessions as both mentor and mentee.

- To create a playground for creativity, banter and delight. Some sessions are somber and dark because the story takes the conversation there; some sessions are filled with laughter, humor and feel more like the playground than battlefield. The right environment for mentoring is a space that welcomes a sense of play even in the hardest work

The momentum of spiritual mentoring will always depend on the ongoing living work of the Holy Spirit. This is where some readers begin to panic or even lose interest. "I don't know what it means to listen to the Spirit. I have enough trouble listening to the mentee; how do I know it is God to whom I am listening anyway and not just my own self?" Through prayerful trust and trustful waiting.

- Prayer preceded your selection of a mentee and precedes every session with the mentee. It is active and intercessory on behalf of the mentee's spiritual well-being.

- Prayer is the practice that begins your session with the mentee. Aloud and conscious or not, prayer is your request for capacity to hear the voice of the Spirit in your work together.

- Prayerful trust is when you "seek first the kingdom (of God) and his righteousness" with a grateful heart. Trust is your own humility before God that acknowledges you might not get it right. Brennan Manning wasn't timid when he wrote about gratitude. He called it "ruthless trust." "The foremost quality of a trusting disciple is gratefulness. Gratitude arises from the lived perception, evaluation and acceptance of all of life as grace—as an undeserved and unearned gift from the Father's hand. Such recognition is itself the work of grace, and acceptance of the gift is implicitly an acknowledgment of the Giver."[3]

SLOW DOWN

That kind of trust leads to waiting on the Spirit of the Lord. Waiting is not a passive moment of detachment but an active exercise of trust. Like a pregnant woman waits on the birth of her child, the mentor waits on the Spirit. Trustful waiting is hard work because we too easily jump to conclusions. Possibly the greatest threat for the mentor is to take over the work and move to conclusions, answers, solutions and resolution. This is slow work—painfully slow at times. It requires more than patience; it requires deep enough trust to wait on the Spirit of the Lord to speak, move, nudge, infuse hope, encourage, touch and love.

Pace isn't about speed; in spiritual mentoring it is about movement, sometimes a movement to slow down. Across the centuries, our best spiritual teachers all seemed to understand that. Earlier generations lived connected to the rhythms of daylight, seasons and the slow growth of crops. They didn't just understand such things; they knew them because they lived the rhythms. That's why biblical spirituality creates rhythms of daily prayer, weekly Sabbath and continuous pilgrimage. It can't be said too often: momentum is about listening and seeing, discerning God's intentions for your work together. The nature of spiritual guidance needs to be consistent with the nature of spirituality itself: God takes the lead. As mentor, my job is to follow. Momentum in the holy work of spiritual mentoring is listening with a responsive heart.

How is trust established? In the same way it is established between friends. Through honest conversation, risks, shared life, playful enjoyment and time. In true friendship, trust is almost certainly tested, which means that trust is sustained only as we learn to start over when trust has been shaken or lost. Who is the person you trust with your most intimate secrets? How did that relationship move to that level of trust? I would guess you took some risks with each other and found the other to have integrity. I would guess there was a mutual sharing of ideas, thoughts, experiences and stories, and that some of those conversations included themes of pain, suffering, loss, trauma and heartbreak. Relationships generally don't become trustful without shadows and darkness. "All sunshine makes a desert" isn't a mindless quip; all sunshine doesn't make a trusting relationship. Most of us develop trust with another in fits and starts, stuttering speech and clumsy attempts at being present to one another. It isn't a science; it's a covenantal, relational, spiritual art. My best mentors have said to me things like, "I don't have any idea where we go next." "I have never had an experience like yours, but I want to feel what you did in it." "I want to understand; please say it again another way." This is not the rhetoric of technicians but of caring people who have longed to be present to me.

"Be here now" said someone along my journey. What if that's the primary work of the mentor? *To be*—not only to speak and give answers but *to be here*; in other words, to be present to my story and *to be here now*, in this moment. It takes hard work to be here now. So many things call me away from this present moment in my story—my past, my longings for the future, my desires, my temptations, my inner storyteller, and distractions of sight, sound and sense. It takes hard work to stay attuned to another person and to listen. But you know what it feels like when someone is fully present with you. You know what it feels like to be listened to with that kind of depth. It is like fresh air, fresh water, healing balm and saving grace. It happens too seldom for most of us.

The mentee must simply show up, not only in body but in spirit, heart and readiness. Nurturing a sustained relationship is a two-way street. The mentor will create questions and assignments and set a framework for the relational work of mentoring, but the mentee will bring his or her own energy, engagement and preparation. All relationships require care and continued attention. And just as in friendship, there is not a single list of rules for the nurture of the relationship, but it does require an intentionality on the part of the mentee to also be here now.

You show up ready to listen, to be curious, to wonder and to engage; you show up ready to read your life as story. Such reading may include furious frustration and anger: "That can't be true, can it?" Or "I don't want that to be my story; how do you see that in me?" It may come in a gentle openness to sit in silence and wait. It may come in rapid-fire questions to a mentor. It may come in a prayerful mode of attention. The distinguishing quality is a readiness for formation, guidance and direction. What is the opposite of readiness? A closed mind, a heart that is unwilling to listen, a spirit that is preoccupied. When I am preoccupied, I am literally already occupied; I already have answers, solutions, information, and am neither ready nor willing to learn. The unteachable spirit already has concluded they know what they need to know or have lost interest in the quest. Sustaining momentum is dependent on the readiness and responsiveness of the mentee.

Did you know in the world of neuroscience there are people who have become "distraction experts"? In her book *Now You See It: How the Brain Science of Attention Will Transform the Way We Live, Work, and Learn*, Dr. Cathy Davidson lets us in on what science has discovered about paying attention: "Attention begins in the nursery, but as we age, we also learn to shape and reshape the values we learn there. Learning is the cartography of cultural value, indistinguishable from the landscape of our attention—and our blindness."[4] And she says, "To live is to be in a constant state of adjustment. We can change by accident—because we have to, because life throws us a curveball. But we can also train ourselves to be aware of our own neural processing—repetition, selection, mirroring—and arrange our lives so we have the tools *and the partners to help us see what we might miss on our own.*"[5]

The mentor will become that partner in learning to pay attention. Distraction, says Davidson, is something to which we should pay attention. "Distraction can help us pinpoint areas where we need to pay more attention, where there is a mismatch between our knee-jerk reactions and what is called for in the situation at hand. If we can think of distraction as an early warning signal, we can become aware of processes that are normally invisible to us."[6] The new brain studies help us focus our spiritual work. We are able to read more than one thing at a time—we can read the story of the mentee and listen carefully to our instincts and the nudges of the Spirit. We can listen well to the distractions of the mentee as an early warning signal of more to come and start to work on those topics.

RESPONSIVE ENGAGEMENT

I walked with a nationally known pastoral leader from the college to the seminary across the hill. He was on his way to speak to a group of pastors gathered by the faculty. "How do you prepare to speak to a group of leaders you've never met before?" I asked him.

"They are leaders. It's easy to speak to leaders. I always speak to their hearts because they are some of the neediest people I know."

"How can that be?" I wanted to know.

"Because they find it harder than most to remain open, teachable, willing to listen."

As a leader and pastor, I knew he told the truth. I confess that I know it too well in myself. It isn't that I want to close my heart to growth, but I have often lived behind the mask of my positions or roles. I have sometimes allowed the perception of my wisdom or the authority of my role to shut me off from my own readiness to listen. And I have received the gift of *anamchara* from friends willing to speak truth into my life.

Jay, university president and leader but my mentor—he had much to offer. His questions somehow invited me to something rather than cajoled me into it. His questions welcomed me to the table rather than critiqued me once I got there. His questions called out something from me that he believed to be there rather than judged me for what he knew I did not yet know. His questions invited me to a place of courage and confidence. I'd like to believe I have done that for others.

Jesus spoke with uncompromising clarity about the need for a teachable spirit. On this particular day he did as he often did: he told stories called parables that confused some and motivated others to ask questions. Readiness and receptive insight—that's a teachable spirit. His words to his friends were an announcement about how to walk with him on the journey of the spirit.

The disciples came up and asked, "Why do you tell stories?"

He replied, "You've been given insight into God's kingdom. You know how it works. Not everybody has this gift, this insight; it hasn't been given to them. Whenever someone has a ready heart for this, the insights and understandings flow freely. But if there is no readiness, any trace of receptivity soon disappears. That's why I tell stories: to create readiness, to nudge the people toward receptive insight. In their present state they can stare till doomsday and not see it, listen till they're blue in the face and not get it. I don't want Isaiah's forecast repeated all over again:

Your ears are open but you don't hear a thing.
    Your eyes are awake but you don't see a thing.
The people are blockheads!
They stick their fingers in their ears
    so they won't have to listen;
They screw their eyes shut
    so they won't have to look,
    so they won't have to deal with me face-to-face
    and let me heal them.

"But you have God-blessed eyes—eyes that see! And God-blessed ears—ears that hear! A lot of people, prophets and humble believers among them, would have given anything to see what you are seeing, to hear what you are hearing, but never had the chance." (Matthew 13:10-17 *The Message*)

How the Mentee Prepares for Each Session

Mentoring is not a solo task conducted by the mentor alone; it is relational work that involves preparation by the mentee as well. Assignments are often the most obvious preparation, but I also find there are questions a mentee can ask themselves that focus on "getting ready" or "being ready."

Questions a mentee might ask themselves as they prepare for mentoring include:

- How much of myself am I willing to bring to our time today?

- Am I ready to be present in body, heart and spirit?

- Can I set aside the distractions of the day or bring them as necessary chapters in my story?

- Is there debris in my life that clutters the pathway and limits my ability to listen?

- What helps me discipline my spirit to listen well?

- Can I bring readiness and receptive insight today?

- Have I prepared myself with prayer?

I place major emphasis on the readiness of mentees because their story will become the content for the mentoring session. They must be willing to engage responsively with a teachable spirit, to show up and show up again. As a brief excursus, I want to be direct with those seeking mentoring.

Remember to bring your questions, along with the assignments you've been given. Don't miss how important your questions may be as guides for the next conversation with your mentor. This is why many purchase a journal to use as a simple discipline to jot down at least three things:

1. Questions that won't let you go. Perhaps your mentor asked it for the first time or it came from reading elsewhere, but it seems to hang around and won't let you go. Questions about honest and fearful uncertainty, doubts and bold faith. Questions that linger.

2. Sightings of the kingdom that cause you to exclaim to yourself, *Look, there is the kingdom of God, present in my home, my family, at work, in my neighborhood, on my commute or in pain, confusion, and struggles* or to ask, *What am I looking at?*

3. "Whispers of immortality," as T. S. Eliot called it in his poetry— hints of conviction, new insights and places of growing confidence in the formation of your faith. Elijah heard God not in earthquake and wind or fire but in what has come to be called "the still, small voice of God," which comes as nudges, hints, whispers and questions (1 Kings 19:12-13).

Remember that momentum involves give and take; there is a dynamic of relational energy between you and your mentor. Come to your appointed times prepared by prayer that precedes the meeting. Reflect on the time elapsed since you met. The reading material for this course is your life—it's as simple and profound as that. Don't underestimate the likelihood that God has already given you the reading material for the next session.

You were motivated to seek out mentoring in the beginning because something prompted you to start a relationship with your mentor. Return to that instinct and initial prompting from time to time to keep before you the memory of what you were looking for when you started. Let that memory rekindle your motivation.

Be honest with your mentor as your energy ebbs and flows in the relationship. Don't underestimate that this is hard work and will cost you energy, time and, most importantly, focus. Remember that focus, attention, honesty and curiosity are what you bring to each session. Your role is not passivity; your mentor will help you learn to read, but you bring the reading material as you bring the story of your life.

Remember what Paul said to Timothy, his young mentee, as he coached him with words of constancy, calling him to stay disciplined: "Train yourself in godliness.... Put these things into practice, devote yourself to them, so that all may see your progress" (1 Timothy 4:7, 15). He continued, "Fight the good faith of the faith; take hold of the eternal life, to which you were called and for which you made the good confession in the presence of many witnesses" (1 Timothy 6:12) and, "Guard the good treasure entrusted to you, with the help of the Holy Spirit living in us" (2 Timothy 1:14). And finally:

> But as for you, continue in what you have learned and firmly believed, knowing from whom you learned it, and how from childhood you have known the sacred writings that are able to instruct you for salvation through faith in Christ Jesus. All scripture is inspired by God and is useful for teaching, for reproof, for correction, and for training in righteousness, so that everyone who belongs to God may be proficient, equipped for every good work. (2 Timothy 3:14-17)

Spiritual Mentoring as Prayer

It goes without saying that mentoring is a form of prayer. We engage in conversation and dialogue with another in the presence of the Spirit. As we pray in intercession, we focus on the lives and stories of others. In adoration, we acknowledge the awesome presence of the Almighty before whom our work is conducted. In thanksgiving, we come together to cocreate new chapters with God, the ultimate Author of our story. As supplicants, we boldly ask for God's wisdom and insight for what we need in the moment. In contemplation, we wait on the Spirit of the Lord to open our ears and eyes.

Prayer is simple speech, and in mentoring, clear, honest, direct and simple words are the best vocabulary for formation. So prayer is a metaphor for mentoring—both the practices of prayer and the many ways we pray. Richard Foster's book on prayer lists twenty-one different forms prayer may take. There are prayers that take us inward, upward and outward.[1] Foster writes, "God has graciously allowed me to catch a glimpse into his heart. . . . Today the heart of God is an open wound of love. . . . He longs for our presence."[2] Not surprisingly, the list is incomplete—there is more to prayer than he or any of us knows how to describe because prayer is relationship with this triune God who longs for our presence.

And there is more: prayer is the actual environment in which we seek righteousness and formation. It is a place, not only a practice or set of practices. In prayer we know ourselves in the liminal space between God and humankind. I started this book with a reference to Thomas Kelley, who described the inner place as a sanctuary of the soul. It is a way of being in the world. Prayer is not only what we do when we intend to speak to God; it is a way of living in time and place in trustful knowledge that the universe is, in fact, a spiritual reality that God inhabits. I love the study of mysticism and my time with monastics, but I don't live in a hermitage. My spirituality is the spirituality of children, my commute, household and job. Where is prayer in that world? My childhood songs and words spoke of "Jesus in my heart" and later of "My heart, Christ's home." Aside from the many comical questions children ask about Jesus' comfort within their small body, the metaphors helped me understand that Jesus was with me. Where I went, Jesus went. Where I lived, Christ lived. Prayer is not a religious act so much as a human conversation in the midst of waking, walking, working, loving, searching, losing, finding, confessing, denying, longing, yearning, desiring. Wherever I am, prayer is the environment in which I practice my faith. Only I actually had it backwards—where God is, I go. In prayer we recognize that we live in the presence of the living God. Where I go, God is already present. Where I live, God preceded. In typical North American style, I might have gotten it turned around.

One of the great pray-ers I know is my friend Paul. He loves to pray, I think. Prayer is how he lives, not only what he does in religious moments. He loves to pray in the words that come from ancient spiritualties: "With beauty before me, behind me, and all around, we go to a holy place indeed." Prayer is not an activity; prayer is the place in which the activities reside. Prayer is not saying certain words in a religious fashion; it is an awareness of presence all around us and within. Jesus' prayer for the disciples is a formulaic and organized practice of going to that place. In my church we say, "And now as Jesus taught us, we are bold to say . . ." And we recognize that prayer is paying attention to the presence of God in all things. Prayer is a way of being in a world that God inhabits.

10

Sustaining Momentum
Through Accountability

☙

The practices that shaped Jesus' life surprise me until I remember he was a first-century Jew—a people with a spirituality of time and place. His life was organized around certain practices, which were forms of accountability built into the structures of daily life and the home. Spirituality for him included daily practices (*Shema*), weekly practices (Sabbath), symbolic rituals (festivals and pilgrimage) and physical symbols (phylacteries). His house had a *mezuzah* on the front door—a small visual icon that contained a small section of Scripture, the Torah. He prayed as often as five times each day and took a Sabbath every seven days. It is accurate to say he lived in a culture of accountability and discipline. Spiritual formation requires practice. Practice is a form of accountability—to a team, coach, sport or discipline. Physicians "practice" medicine, which means they are accountable for their discipline. Therapists can have a private "practice," which means they are licensed and certified—accountable.

Sustaining momentum in mentoring will likewise require accountability. The work of the mentor is to create exercises or assignments that move the mentee toward accountability.

Momentum is sustained in the mentoring process through accountability, what I like to call "exercises of grace."[1] Through the prayer and thoughtfulness of the mentor, a mentee is given assignments that will typically be discussed in a future session. Such exercises look like ordinary practices to the untrained eye. What I mean by that is that accountability may be as simple as doing what you already do in ordinary practices of your life. But you may do them with renewed intentionality and attention. One of my students is taking an independent study on spirituality from me. He drives two hours each way to our campus. As we crafted the coursework for him, I asked him what he does as he drives. And then I suggested that he use that time for reflective prayer. It didn't require a grand sacrifice on his part or a major time commitment—it found a space in the living of his life for the purpose of spiritual growth. It may not demand a painful "discipleship sacrifice" but instead may be an ordinary "discipleship moment" in the daily routine of life.

The purpose of assignments is to extend the conversations begun in the mentoring session. They create additional and repeated opportunities for the mentee to continue the work started in a mentoring session. After my knee replacement surgery I spent time with Kelly, my neighborhood physical therapist. If I thought my work would be completed in our appointments, I was mistaken. He had assignments for me with handouts, printouts and accountability. He expected me to be engaged between our sessions, not because he wanted me to continue to hurt but rather because he knew that my healing would be aided by daily practice. It's not a complicated concept. Healing and growth don't take place by an appointment at the PT office once a month. New joints need to be exercised, tendons and muscles need to be restored, and scar tissue needs to be kept from taking over the surgical area. In the same way, mentoring assignments extend the work beyond a weekly or monthly session. For the mentee, assignments extend the time for sustained reflection; they are the way things get done.

We often make it more complicated than it needs to be. If Jesus' life is a good example, the religious disciplines were immersed into the routines and rhythms of daily life. You took them to work with you, and they were waiting when you arrived home. When Eugene Peterson translated the *Shema* of Deuteronomy 6 in *The Message*, he wrote:

> Write these commandments that I've given you today on your hearts. Get them inside of you and then get them inside your children. Talk about them wherever you are, sitting at home or walking in the street; talk about them from the time you get up in the morning to when you fall into bed at night. Tie them on your hands and foreheads as a reminder; inscribe them on the doorposts of your homes and on your city gates. (Deuteronomy 6:6-9 *The Message*)

This doesn't sound as if religion is somehow apart from where I live, what I do and how I spend my time. These practices become exercises of grace because they are a reminder; they are a reminder because they are inscribed inside of us. Over time people have called them spiritual disciplines or spiritual practices; they are exercises in accountability for the sake of formation. The best assignments become embedded in daily routines and habitual practices like those described in the Deuteronomy 6 text. What Moses gave to his community was tactile, pragmatic, visual, repeated and practical. Spirituality in ancient Israel was not meant to be *apart* from the life of home, house, family and work, but embodied and embedded, even visually in places you see every day and in activities you practice every day. Not an exhaustive list, these accountability assignments might provoke you as mentor to create your own growing list of spiritual assignments. In one way or another, all of these accountability exercises enable the mentor to help keep a mentee accountable for their own practices of attention. I need my alarm clock to call me to attention to the morning. I need the chimes to ring at my school to remind me of God's presence as they ring at nine, noon and three. I need accountability, in others, to do what Benedict said was the starting place: listen.

Everyone can find a few minutes in the day to reflect on what has happened, what questions have been asked, what you have longed for, desired, feared or wondered. I suggest you start with as little as ten minutes in a day to *write in a journal*. If you are a morning person, write as you drink your coffee or tea to start the day; if you are able, some write on a break at work, and many work best at the end of the day.

At the Seattle School of Theology and Psychology, the chimes ring at nine, noon and three to remind us audibly that our lives are lived and our work is done in the presence of the living God. It works as it is intended—it interrupts my train of thought and reminds me that I do my work in the presence of another, the living God. A common exercise is to ask people to *remember to pray every day*—if possible on their commute to work or as they sit at a desk or stand at a workstation to begin the day. Smartphones with their alarm clocks can be scheduled to provide similar chimes of reminder to pray. Sometimes I assign prayers of compassion and attention for others. "Pray for people you meet or see each day: strangers, coworkers, family or friends." Most often I don't ask people to pray for themselves but to practice contemplative prayers of listening or prayers for others. Sometimes I invite people to memorize the Lord's Prayer and repeat it at least three times in their day.

The Jesus Prayer is one of our most important historical prayers. As you breathe in you say the first words, "Lord Jesus Christ," and as you exhale you say the final words, "have mercy on me, a Sinner." This is a prayer that can be practiced throughout the day.

Scriptural repetition is one way to listen to what God says of his love for people. Typically I ask people to read a text every day for at least thirty days. "There is therefore now no condemnation for those who are in Christ Jesus" (Romans 8:1) is one such text. "Remember, I am with you always, to the end of the age" (Matthew 28:20) is another, as is "God saw everything that he had made, and indeed, it was very good" (Genesis 1:31). The texts are usually in stark contrast to the words mentees tell themselves; the repetition will inscribe an alternative on their mind, memory and soul.

Children exercises are practices that invite a parent to "recite" these things to your children. It can be a reflection time with your child in which you take the lead about where you heard God speak today. It may be in reading a story that invites thoughtful contemplation with your child about how God is alive in the world. It could be an invitation to find a way to give a daily blessing to your children as they prepare to lie down or as they rise for the day ahead.

Lectio divina is a particular form of spiritual reading. It asks you to listen for the voice of God in texts rather than to read for information. It is a way of reading that invites reflection. Like a cow chewing its cud, *lectio divina* is a slow way of reading to hear or sense God's voice. Appendix one outlines a simple method for the practice of *lectio divina.*

Letters are meant to be written, though not always sent. I remember an early experience as a new, young faculty member and campus pastor. I was outraged at something that happened (or didn't happen) in a faculty meeting, and I wrote longhand a four-page letter that detailed my unhappiness with my colleagues.

Thankfully, I shared it with my president, whose wisdom saved the day. "Keith, I agree with you. Your insights are accurate, your anger is appropriate, and your analysis is correct; of course, you cannot send this letter." That day I learned the accountability of putting thoughts, feelings and passion in words and the wisdom, that day at least, to not launch my thoughts for all the campus to hear. Sometimes these letters are burned, buried or safeguarded in a journal for confidentiality. Mentees will frequently need to confess, confront or fiercely lament a moment in their story. Writing the letter puts words to the story; reading the letter aloud to the mentor imprints the words in a new moment in their story.

Silence is a particularly difficulty exercise for most outgoing people. Relationships are what drives them, so the specter of thirty minutes in silence feels more like a punishment than grace. It is T. S. Eliot's words about silence from his poem "Ash Wednesday" that captivate me most: "Where shall the word be found, where will the word Resound? Not here, there is not enough silence."[2] The silence exercise requires the mentee to spend a designated amount of time without words or sound. It is often puzzling to mentees that I think silence will "do" anything for them, but across the long history of Christian spirituality, silence is known to be one of our most powerful teachers. As the psalmist wrote, "Be still and know that I am God" (Psalm 46:10).

Solitude and retreats are assignments for those with sufficient time and resources. When mentees can find time and access to solitude and retreat centers, monastic settings or private space, new horizons often open for them. A young friend returned recently from three days in the desert on a retreat in solitude. He was changed somehow by the experience and he knew it, although he couldn't explain how it worked on him. He read, prayed and listened to his soul in a wild place along with others on a similar journey to solitude.

Readings often include Scripture texts but may be poetry, fiction or prose. I often will ask a mentee to read the same text each day for seven, fourteen or twenty-one days to break through to a deep enough ability to hear what has become blocked in them. A friend of mine, a university pastor, told me he read the works of the same spiritual teacher for five years. He pared down his reading of many voices and chose to focus on the writings of one. That one was Thomas Merton, one of our most profound spiritual teachers. On my short list of writers you will find Wendell Berry's fiction and poetry, Barbara Brown Taylor's sermons, Frederick Buechner's memoirs, Annie Dillard's writings (all of them), Henry Nouwen's teaching, Flannery O'Connor's short stories and everything written by Eugene Peterson.

Questions often emerge in a mentoring session and remain unanswered in that time. I assign the question to be asked, written about and pondered until we meet for our next session. Simple or complex, the questions are an invitation to mentees to read the story of their life through their own yet-to-be-answered questions, doubts or thoughts. I'm not looking for them to find answers but to learn to listen to their own life through sustained contemplation of the questions that pursue them. They are as simple as reflection questions on the highs and lows of the week or as deep as the question from our African friends, "Are you at peace?" They are as general as "What do you hear God saying as you pray?" or as specific as "Why do you think the topic we've been working through stirs emotion for you?"

Father exercises are usually assigned only after a long season of trust has developed. Sometimes these are letters written never to be sent. Sometimes, however, they are written, edited, rewritten and sent. It is not unusual that many of us find our understanding of God commingled in the confusion, joy, delight, pain, sorrow and heartbreak of our relationship with our own father. Mentors know they spend a large amount of time in conversations about fathers when the mentee is really talking about God, and, conversely, about God when they're really trying to make sense of their fathers. It seems we all want to make sense out of our relationships with fathers and mothers. I typically ask the mentee to read the letter aloud to me; most break down in emotions before they can finish. Most find such exercises painfully healing.

I don't know when I started to create assignments of *service*, but I have found that many get stuck because they are overly occupied with reflection on themselves. The great danger in counseling, spiritual direction, spiritual mentoring, contemplative prayer and meditation is that all of these can lead us to obsess about ourselves. For many of us, the way out is to find a practical way to serve others and get our minds off ourselves long enough to remember that the church is sent to the places where the world is in pain.[3] Freedom can often be found in service given to others in small, practical and repeated practice.

Sometimes I invite people to forge or craft a *pillar of memory*. It is described in 1 Samuel 7:12 where God answered Samuel's prayer for help and he erected a pillar of memory, an Ebenezer, or a stone of assistance to memorialize this time when God's love was manifested. Simple or elaborate, artful or crude, the point of the exercise is to create a physical pillar of stones to remind one of a moment when God's presence was seen or felt. A pillar of memory may literally be a collection of stones, but it might just as well be a photograph, poem, song, prayer or story.

Conversations with a spouse or household member. Spiritual mentoring can become a practice of secrets withheld from a spouse or other household members, which can actually create walls or barriers between two loved ones. The exercise is simply to invite the mentee to create a conversation in which a part of the work being done with the mentor is shared. The tricky part of such conversations is timing. Sometimes the work that most needs to be done is related to issues with a spouse, which require more focus and listening with the mentor. Sometimes, however, the mentee has come to find a safe place for intimacy with a mentor that can dangerously replace spiritual intimacy in the home or household. Wise attention to those with whom the mentee lives is essential. Timing for such an assignment requires wisdom. Since the spouse or household member didn't sign up for mentoring, this assignment will need to come as an invitation or request from the mentee.

In many religious homes in an earlier time, the day ended with a child kneeling next to the bed in prayer. The imagery of Jesus on his knees next to a stone in the desert or the Garden of Gethsemane may be the source of this practice, but there was something rhythmic about ending the day in an exercise of examination of the day. For me, that exercise was a time of reflection on my sins so that I might confess. *The examen* is a practice most frequently associated with Ignatius of Loyola. A current Ignatian website describes five steps in the practice of daily examen:

- Become aware of God's presence.
- Review the day with gratitude.
- Pay attention to your emotions.
- Choose one feature of the day and pray from it.
- Look toward to tomorrow.[4]

The rhythm within the practice is compelling. It doesn't start with a look backwards; it starts with awareness of the present moment.

It grounds us in attention to this time and place: become aware of God's presence. Then it gives instructions for a review of the day, but the qualifying words are necessary: review *with gratitude*. Rather than a review that is critical of behavior, motives and failures, the examen is an exercise in gratitude that invites us to choose one moment, event or experience and focus on that one thing. Rather than a long list of failures, the discipline gets us to focus. We are a distracted people, most of us; our busyness may be an escape from our own souls. I had the unusual opportunity for a sabbatical leave from my work. I rather proudly told my mentor that I planned to take a three-day retreat in silence as a point of focus for my sabbatical. He said, "No, you need to take an eight-day retreat." We bantered back and forth as I told him three days was sufficient. He stopped me in my tracks when he asked, "Why are you so afraid to be alone with the Lord?" I knew the answer: my busyness was my escape. I spent eight days outside of San Francisco on retreat.

The Book of Common Prayer includes liturgies for morning and evening worship. Some are helped by the structure and guidance of the liturgies.[5] The Book of Common Prayer outlines steps for personal and communal worship.

Daily devotions on smartphones are available from many of our important spiritual teachers. Two that I read daily are from Henri Nouwen and Richard Rohr, available at www.henrinouwen.org and https://cac.org/richard-rohr/daily-meditations.

Ignatian disciplines are often structured around *guided reflection*. Whether as a twenty-four-hour, three-day or eight-day retreat, or four-session guided reflection over time, Ignatius believed in the need for exercise.

By the term "Spiritual Exercises" is meant every method of examination of conscience, of meditation, of contemplation, of vocal and mental prayer. . . . For just as taking a walk, journeying on foot, and running are bodily exercises, so we call Spiritual Exercises every way of preparing and disposing the soul to rid itself of all inordinate attachments, and, after their removal, of seeking and finding the will of God in the disposition of our life for the salvation of our soul.[6]

One of the significant contributions from the Ignatian disciplines is the need for guided times of reflection. Careful, reflective thinking is a regular part of effective spiritual mentoring. This is not the only possible way to use reflection as a regular discipline, but its intentionality and structure make it a good one. What Ignatius of Loyola wanted for his directees was a way to look with disciplined eyes. He created four stages for reflection and retreat. Each of these four can be used as part of a retreat, a weekly assignment or a mentoring session all on its own. There is a spatial imagery to this work.

- We need to *look back* at what has been in order to "find God in all things." Through spiritual examen, reflection and the prayers of memory for the day, we can look at what has been.

- There is also a sacramental view through our life to know Jesus more and love him more deeply. Viewing sacramentally is a way of *looking through* to see the deepest thing.

- There is a *looking into* the suffering of Jesus

- Finally, there is a *looking ahead* to resurrection and Easter redemption.

Ignatius wanted to use the spiritual exercises to open our eyes to see God as we look back (memory and recall) and forward (imagination and vision), alongside (with others), around (in community and neighbor) and inside (contemplative reflection).[7]

Sometimes in the Protestant church we make too much of the ecclesial connection for practices we will adopt. If they are monastic, Roman Catholic or Orthodox rather than Protestant, we are suspicious. In that limited perspective we might lose an entire rich history of sources for spiritual guidance and centuries of tested spiritual practices.

In the end, accountability is one way we extend the mentoring session for the mentee. As the work develops over time, there is often a longing for more. Like good nutrition, the spiritual nourishment of a healthy mentoring relationship fuels the mentee forward. I can give witness from my own times with my seminary professor Dan, or with Gloria, William, Jay, John or Brennan. I was slowly being transformed in a process that was not always or even often visible or tangible to me. But the measures I could identity were increased curiosity, awareness, questions, disillusionment, intimacy with the Spirit and a hunger for more. You can read the list again and see that accountability doesn't translate into linear growth, perfection or ascent, but to more of life.

Spiritual Mentoring
as Geography

I was first introduced to the concept of spiritual mentoring as geography when I lived in the prairies of South Dakota. I was drawn, not surprisingly, to Kathleen Norris's book *Dakota: A Spiritual Geography*.[1] Norris and her husband moved from New York City to Lemmon, South Dakota, to sell her grandparents' home. To their surprise, they remained there for over two decades and learned about the land, landscape and geography as powerful metaphors for spirituality. The editor writes of the book, "In thoughtful, discerning prose, she explores how we come to inhabit the world we see, and how that world also inhabits us. Her voice is a steady assurance that we can, and do, chart our spiritual geography wherever we go.[2]

In my own first experience with spiritual direction, I was assigned a reading in the Gospel of Mark with these directions: "Read until something causes you to stop." I made it to chapter one, verse four, where John the Baptist was wandering around in the wilderness. The location stopped me dead in my tracks; it compelled to think about spirituality in terms of place, location and geography. My seminary education emphasized a more ethereal, otherworldly and eternal understanding, someplace other than here and now. The word *geography*, Norris points out, has to do with land, so her writing about the relatively isolated and barren landscape of Dakota was a way to find coherence and meaning in her life.

Jesus' life was lived in the geography of at least five kinds of spaces: desert, mountains, water (sea and river), gardens and cities. Alone and with others, isolated and in community, in moments of epiphany and grief, Jesus seemed to live aware of where he was and how it shaped him. The language of spiritual geography is suggestive of time and place. We each have times in the desert or wilderness. We feel the isolation and rugged solitude as either healing or barren. There are mountain experiences like Jesus had with Moses and Elijah, Peter and John, when we feel the presence of God as epiphany. There is also the loneliness, darkness and hugeness of the mountain experience. When my sister-in-law Sharon was dying of breast cancer, she spoke about her love of scuba diving and time on the waters of Puget Sound as a womb-like experience in a cocoon of beauty, surprise, color and life. But she also knew loneliness as she spoke of feeling like a small boat on the vast waters of the sea. Gardens can be places of beauty and life; for Jesus they could be a place of testing, as Gethsemane was a garden for making decisions about facing the epic battle of the cross. Cities were, for him, also places of conflict, confrontation and eventually death. A small-town boy, more familiar with the countryside of Judea than the urban center of Jerusalem, Jesus moved between places of presence and voice. What does spiritual geography suggest for the mentor?

• It is a way to offer an invitation for the mentee to locate their story in time and place, not just as detail but as metaphor for times of emotion, presence, absence or experience.

- It is a way to remind us that our lives are shaped by neighborhoods, neighbors and strangers. Spirituality is not "out there" in disembodied reality but here and now in places we live and visit.

- It is a way to teach the mentee to pay attention to the present. Margaret Guenther writes, "Two of my favorite holy places are the subway and the kitchen, although both could be seen as spiritually empty, waste places. The subway, where we cannot escape the sight of the wounded Body of Christ, is a fruitful place for prayers of intercession, while repetitive tasks in the kitchen can be sanctified by the Jesus Prayer." ("Jesus Christ, God's Son, have mercy on me.") [3]

Ending Well

"You have been given questions to which you cannot be given answers. You will have to live them out—perhaps a little at a time."

"And how long is that going to take?"

"I don't know. As long as you live, perhaps."

"That could be a long time."

"I will tell you a further mystery," he said. "It may take longer."[1]

Rules don't dictate relationships. Relationships are human, which means the unexpected can happen just as easily as the planned. Maybe that's why this chapter is the hardest to write. It's one thing to list out rules for ending well or guidelines for closure, but the story of an ending most likely has its own beginning, middle and ending, as does the story itself because it is the experience of relationship over time.

THE BEGINNING OF THE ENDING

When the young Jayber Crow met with his teacher, Dr. Ardmire, he became a mentee. He brought his life, which was full of questions, and the wise old professor became a mentor who gave no answers but pointed him in a direction. "You will have to live them out—perhaps a little at a time." Ending well does not mean the questions have all been answered, the problems solved and the issues sorted out. Ending well is not a closure for the mentee; it is substantively the turning of the page and the start of a new chapter. Ending well is sometimes the muddiest part of the mentoring process; something will prompt or necessitate the ending of the work between mentor and mentee.

- Some endings are created on purpose and timed with wise discernment and planning.

- Some sadly drift into unfinished endings.

- Some are abrupt, created by unexpected transitions.

- Some end in emotional collisions, in uncertainty, frustration or anger.

PLANNING TO END WELL

In mountain climbing, I was trained to practice what we called a shakedown. (Coming from Chicago, a shakedown meant something different than in the Cascade Mountains.) About an hour after the hike begins, the group takes time to stop and evaluate progress, adjust loads, and check on questions of pace, pain and expectations. Frequently ropes, tents or shared equipment will be transferred to someone with a lighter load or balanced more carefully among the team. We ask questions about very practical things, like blisters, layers of clothing, sunscreen, water, food and shoes.

- Are the shoes too tight? Did they get tied well?

- Are you getting too warm with the layers, or do you need another layer because of wind, cold or rain?

- Are you keeping hydrated? Do you need to eat?
- How is the pace for you? Are we going too fast for someone to keep up?
- Does anyone have pain in toes, feet, legs or shoulders?
- What are your expectations for the rest of the day? Are you surprised by anything? Are there questions you need to ask about the route, trail or path?

All of these questions in a shakedown are intended to set a trajectory for a successful climb. I remember an early experience on a climb when I was given both a full rope and a group tent. My boots were relatively new, and I needed to add another layer of socks to keep them from starting to blister, but I was not going to slow down the whole group for my own physical comfort. When the group leader called for a halt and explained the purpose of the shakedown, I discovered I was not the only one in need of adjustments. It's not hard to make the transfer to a shakedown after a few weeks in the mentoring experience. A few sessions of mentoring give enough information for mentor and mentee to ask similar questions about expectations, pace, balance, load and route. It is useful to practice the shakedown and check in with the mentee as a kind of diagnosis of progress. It is also a necessary diagnostic moment to assess when the work of mentoring is gearing down; it creates an opportunity to end well. As a pastor I tried to practice the rule of four when a parishioner suffered the death of a loved one. I tried to make contact with them four days, four weeks and four months after the funeral. Similarly, four sessions and four months are good markers for a shakedown session in mentoring.

THE MIDDLE OF AN ENDING

How do you know it's time to finish the work of mentoring?

1. Continue to ask in shakedown discussions, "How are we doing?" "Is this time meeting the needs we identified at the beginning of our times together?" "Still?" If you set a timeline early in your covenant making, you have built in times to ask in nonthreatening ways, "Are we finished with our work of mentoring?" It can also happen that you agree to meet for a particular length of time and keep closure in sight as the ending date becomes near.

2. Continue a prayerful discernment process. There are various kinds of endings, including natural closure due to the end of the work or graduation, but there are also endings that emerge from dissatisfaction or loss of focus. When the mentor discerns that time is close, enter a season of prayer with the mentee for mutual agreement. This is always relational work, so the best wisdom is to ask each other to diagnose the effectiveness of the work together.

3. If there is a declining motivation, interest or purpose in the work that is recognized by one or both mentor and mentee, it is necessary to make the decline part of the conversation. Asking questions about the decline may become the portal to ending well. One of the surprising questions to ask is, "What might lead us to ending well?" Or, "What would closure for this mentoring relationship look like if we do it well?"

4. If the mentee starts to miss meetings or seems to be adrift, wandering or distracted, it's time to consider if this season of work is over. It requires a conversation together to assess the value and goals for continuing. What sometimes presents itself as distraction and wandering may, however, be the topic most in need of attention. It often moves mentor and mentee into a new and renewed phase of work. Revisiting the covenant created in

the early stages of work can start a new phase of re-energized work. Or it can become a marker that points to closure.

5. If you as the mentor start to find yourself distracted, losing interest or wandering, it's time to take a serious look at the relationship and to ask your own mentor to help you discern the cause(s) of the distraction. Of course, there are other occasions when a mentee simply chooses to move on without a reason.

6. Recognize the signs of a natural closure. The calendar may pragmatically tell you that the school year is over or a season has come to an end. In other words, a natural event will precipitate an expected and natural closure of the season of mentoring. Moving vans are often a clue. If life changes will take a mentor or mentee to another location, the transition work is at hand. As much as is possible, give advance notice and begin to talk through the meaning of endings and closure in what has, hopefully, become a valued relationship.

Abrupt and unplanned closure often leads to painful emotional transitions. Some research suggests that 40 to 60 percent of all mentoring relationships with high school students will end in unexpected closure. They lose interest, life pressures create added stress, emotions are aroused, or life simply takes over and schedules become conflicted. That isn't my experience with college or postgraduate students or with other adults, but experiences do intervene to cause unexpected closure. Mentoring is a voluntary relational process; it's not surprising, then, that people change and circumstances lead to closure, planned and unexpected. In all relationships, endings are times of risk because they can lead to lack of relational closure, disruption, unnecessary loss, feelings of abandonment or betrayal, and unfinished business. When a rupture takes place in the mentoring relationship without relational care and conversation, painful endings ensue. Starting well can set a direction and expectation for ending well, but all relationships are subject to unexpected closure. I believe the mentor takes the larger portion of responsibility to bring good closure, even in an unexpected ending of the work. The greatest threat is usually unfinished business. Because of an unexpected closure, conversations that were in process simply stop abruptly.

ENDINGS ARE TRANSITIONS: HOW TO BRING GOOD CLOSURE

What leads to good closure? How can the mentor minimize the likelihood of unexpected closure or move toward good closure? Good closure is consistent with starting well and creating good momentum—it is intentional, planned and discerning. Start with a covenant that includes a target date for either closure or assessment. While many mentoring relationships continue long-term, there is wisdom in setting a limited number of sessions, weeks or months. After four months it may be time to review and assess expectations, progress and satisfaction. Endings are transitions—they lead to new beginnings—so ending well is also about planning for the next steps for the mentee. What contributes to a good ending? Some review annually after that. In some cases, mentoring relationships last for years; some are more circumstantial and last an academic year or a season in one's life.

Look back. Review what has been, and give both mentor and mentee time to name what has been written in the story of the mentee, first, and in the story of the mentor, second. I believe the greatest failure to end well is in harvesting or gathering. At its best this process is an honest and unvarnished version of chapters written, character developed, plots understood and new directions identified. In many situations it is best for the mentor to take the lead and talk about their impressions of growth. In one situation I remember a decision made to bring a group mentoring experience to a close because it hadn't gone well. When I named my assessment out loud, there was a group sigh of recognition. As much as we wanted to make it work, it hadn't gone well. But we didn't skip the stage of review, and we named good things we had worked on and learned from each other. My wise friend Tom starts most sessions with the question "What did you bring with you *into* the time today?" Likewise, a valuable ending question is "What are you taking with you *out* of our weeks together?"

Look around. Is there any unfinished business for mentor and mentee? Are there concerns or issues that ought to be finished? Were there flare-ups or emotions that remain on the table that ought to be stated and allowed to come to conversation? This is a valuable time for the mentor to ask for honest feedback: "What went well in our work together?" and "What could we have done differently?" Ideally, the latter question is asked in process and not only at the conclusion of the mentoring work. In some cases the mentor and mentee will continue to be friends, socially or in a church or academic setting.

Look ahead. Mentoring when moving transitions are involved often creates the likelihood of a handoff to another mentor. Some mentors I know invite the mentee to write ongoing questions and topics for conversation with a new mentor. For example, "What do you hope to take with you as a starting place in your next mentoring experience?" As always, the focus is on goals and growth for the mentee. The images can abound: an ending is like turning the page to a new chapter. In an ending you merely finish one story as you start to write the next one. Endings for the mentor and mentee are actually transitions for both. Both will move ahead to different relationships in the various stages of transition.

Look with gratitude. Ending well is saying thanks to God. If the format has been one of listening well to the Spirit, how can mentor and mentee celebrate with thanksgiving? What liturgy of gratitude fits the relationship as it has been practiced over weeks or months? Offer prayers of thanks and a benediction for each other. I like to make the sign of the cross on an individual and send them out with the words of the Anglican benediction "Go in peace to love and serve the Lord."

Look within. Naming the experience is a way of telling each other the story of your experience of the other and of your time together. Typically the mentor will take the lead, either by telling their own story of the sessions together or inviting the mentee to put into words their own experience. It is necessary to create safety for both to name positive and negative things, generative and distracting things. The purpose is not to create a grade card for the sessions but rather to name aloud together what has been learned, discerned and heard. In a spirit of honesty and gratitude, both are invited to tell the story of many hours spent in spiritual conversation.

Create symbols to memorialize the time together. I am not creative at this, but I know some mentors who are. Some create works of art separately or together to name the experience and remember it. I have been given pottery made by mentees of various skill levels. Another gave me a candle with words written on a card that said, "Because you taught me to believe in myself more than I could on my own." Books are easier for me to give but must be chosen with thoughtfulness and care. One mentee came to each session with a French Press pot of coffee to share, so it was a natural final session to drink good coffee together as we looked back on almost two years of conversation. Most often the symbols are words or phrases that describe lessons learned, decisions made, and moments shared in the giving and receiving of story.

S/ENDING

In the rhythmic cycles of the academic life comes a season that we call S/Ending. It's not a typo. *Ending* is what happens as the academic calendar runs out of days. *Sending* is what we do as students come to commencement. In the fortunes of vocabulary, the word for graduation is a word that has to do with starting as much as with ending. To commence is not to stop but to start. It just happens to also refer to a ceremony of graduation. At the Seattle School we start the season of S/Ending in February of every year as we prepare students to graduate and to commence. S/Ending is one way we plan to bring closure to the life-transforming experience of education.

Which raises the question "Now what?" What's next? What do you do afterward? One of our most honored employees, Molly, was battling hard against cancer. I talked to her the other day about her final chemo session. She told me something curious: even after a long, frightening, sometimes devastating and always physically demanding regimen of chemotherapy, most cancer patients find themselves filled with angst and loss as the whole thing comes to an end. Community develops in a chemo center. Relationships are built with doctors, nurses and staff. In her case, these were often remarkable people she came to trust. There is a sense of nesting, I should think, as people go through the hard things together. And for my dearly beloved friend there is simply the sense that once something has ended, there needs to be something to do next. She said to me with her wonderful wry smile, "You know me, I need to know about the next project."

In the Episcopal Church, as we end the worship time we often hear these words: "Go in peace to love and serve the Lord." I was part of a small Episcopal congregation in a small rural community, and Karen, our rector, tripped up almost every week on those words. It became a mental block, I suppose, and it became a bit humorous as we waited to see what mixed-up combination of words would come tumbling out. "Go and serve in peace or love." "Love and go." We often were surprised by the new ordering of the words. On one Sunday, two of us were prepared to help our friend and leader. As we finished the service, she stood in the center of the congregation and we held up two signs. Mine said, "Go in peace." The other sign said, "To love and serve the Lord." We had it properly ordered.

If only the going was as orderly as the sending. If only the going could be clarified by holding up the signs with the correct words. If only the sending was a neat and orderly ending. We all know better. Graduate school concludes with words of ending and con-gratulations, pictures are taken to memorialize the moment of ending, and then it's over. But endings are not the end. The edu-cation we confirm in the conferral of degrees had better not be the end of education. I'm pretty sure that about half of what our grad-uates need to know to be a therapist, a pastor, an artist or a leader will only be found in the practice of those things. The medical profession has it right: doctors *practice* medicine—learning every day, hoping to get better at it, deepening the skill and the craft and the art. Ending well does that too. It ensures that the ending of this season of mentoring is not the end but a commencement to some-thing more. Every good ending is always a sending. Finishing a long relationship as a mentor can be emotional as both feel a sense of loss or sadness; it can be awkward as one or both find it hard to say goodbye and end well; it can be difficult if there remains un-finished business. It may also create a deep sense of the spiritual joy both have felt as life has been lived in the presence of the living God. The closure of a long mentoring experience may be especially emotional because of the amount of time shared. It may also feel as natural as life transitions that come at just the right time. And often, there is simply the unanswered question "What's next?"

What I long for as a way of ending well is that we will ask that question. Some will not go on to work with another mentor but some will. Some have started a lifelong practice of keeping a journal and will continue to both write and read their story. Some are eager to find another mentor in the new place, and some will take time out.

I saw a logo on a cement company truck once that read, "Find a hole and fill it." I'm not really sure what that means, but I think it is worthy of some thought. It sounds like it has something to do with vocation and "what's next?" What I want to emphasize in ending well is always about what's next.

William James talked about entering a fight that matters. It's a complicated sentence so you'll have to read carefully. But he makes a point that is urgently needed in this time in the story of humankind. "If this life be not a real fight, in which something is eternally gained for the universe by success, it is no better than a game of private theatricals from which one may withdraw at will. But it *feels* like a real fight."[2]

I love S/Ending because it is our form of the practice of ancient Israel of marking holy moments with pillars or memorials of stone. They paused at moments of transition to mark the moment. Jacob probably did it better and more often than most because he was always on the run, often in trouble and in desperate need of God. At Beth-El, the house of God, he said, "Surely the LORD is in this place—and I did not know it! . . . This is none other than the house of God, and this is the gate of heaven" (Genesis 28:16-17).

Ending well is not about finishing but about starting again. Even as we say thank you for what has been, we are saying, "Go in peace to love and serve the Lord."

Jayber Crow stood on a hillside looking over the place where he had been loved and had learned the most. "I saw that for me, this country would always be populated with presences and absences, presences of absences, the living and the dead. The world as it was would always be a reminder of the world that was and the world that was to come."[3]

Ten Essentials for
the Mentor's Library

The Mountaineers in Seattle created a list many years ago of resources for hiking. They call them "The Ten Essentials" because they are the minimal resources needed for a successful climb to the summit.[1] The following is another list of ten essential resources for the mentor—authors and texts.

Wendell Berry is a Kentucky farmer, poet, environmentalist and novelist. Better than almost anyone, he understands the meaning of place as geography and community. He honors story as a membership of people who live in time and place. Each Sabbath he writes poetry, and for all of his life he has written stories. I have my favorites, but every novel is a treasure in learning to read story. *Jayber Crow: A Novel*, perhaps unintentionally, is one of the great texts on story and the spiritual life as lived by the town barber, orphaned twice as a child.

Eugene Peterson's work, all of it, is an invitation to sit with him at the tables where he learned spirituality. It started with his mother's voice at the Montana family kitchen table where he first heard of Jesus, then moved to the work table of his father's butcher shop where he learned of vocation; from there it moved to the student's table where he honed his skill in hermeneutics, to the preacher's table for a lifetime of opening Scripture and life to congregations, to the professor's table for wise teaching, and, richly, to a writer's table for a lifetime of writing.

> We don't grow and mature in our Christian life by sitting in a classroom and library, listening to lectures and reading books, or going to church and singing hymns and listening to sermons. We do it by taking the stuff of our ordinary lives, our parents and children, our spouses and friends, our workplaces and fellow workers, our dreams and fantasies, our attachments, our easily accessible gratifications, our depersonalizing of intimate relations, our commodification of living truths into idolatries, taking all this and placing it on the altar of refining fire—our God is a consuming fire—and finding it all stuff redeemed for a life of holiness.[2]

Working the Angles: The Shape of Pastoral Integrity most directly addresses the work of spiritual mentoring. *Leap over a Wall: Earthy Spirituality for Everyday Christians* is his best writing about spirituality as we seek to embody our incarnational faith.

Henri J. M. Nouwen was a pastor, professor, writer and spiritual director. *Reaching Out: The Three Movements of the Spiritual Life* is not only a classic; it is a living way of understanding the invitation to know God.

Frederick Buechner wrote *The Sacred Journey* as a memoir of his life and introduces the genre of sacred story in a riveting personal memoir.

Brennan Manning was a Catholic priest, preacher and writer. An alcoholic, he suffered with his illness but found redemption in the relentless love of God. *The Ragamuffin Gospel* is his most honest description of the ragtag army of failed, flawed and finite followers of Jesus.

Barbara Brown Taylor's book *An Altar in the World: A Geography of Faith* offers one of the most thoughtful forays into the sacred and the ordinary.

Pilgrim at Tinker Creek by Annie Dillard may be the best book ever written about how to see with the eyes of wonder, awe and spirituality.

Dan Allender's work on story is exceptional. *To Be Told: God Invites You to Coauthor Your Story* introduces the work of writing the story of faith and life as good as it gets.

The biblical books of Genesis, Colossians and Romans introduce spirituality and narrative as texts that must be read in order to do the work of spiritual mentoring from a biblical perspective.

Margaret Guenther has written *Holy Listening: The Art of Spiritual Direction*, and it still stands as one of the best introductions we have.

Acknowledgments

I have been the recipient of wisdom, care, accountability and love from gifted people over my lifetime. Like a river washing over me, I feel the influence of family, teachers, students, congregants, colleagues, mentors and mentees, and their stories. My indebtedness to people knows almost no limits because these people have walked alongside me, ahead of me, and even some intrepid few have followed along behind me.

Most of you know who you are because you have been part of a great cloud of witnesses who have helped me when I was in need, comforted me when I was in grief, listened as confessors and showed me a way through, taught me what I was sometimes slow to learn, filled me with a contagion to wonder and to learn. You have been the story I have lived. I hesitate to start a list that is long, rich and full of legacy for me because I would need to copy my daily calendars from a lifetime of being mentored by you all.

It can only be acknowledged with the greatest humility: I may have put the words together and crafted this book in its present form, but it was written by the goodness of others who wrote God's story into my life. I have not always been a ready student, sometimes slower to listen and slow to understand, but I know enough to acknowledge my life has been made more generative, joyful and rich from the orchestra of those whose lives I have been honored to join. Your stories have created for us all a membership in time and space.

One person, however, has helped my eyes to see, my ears to hear and my heart to know how fierce love can be: Wendy McJunkin Anderson.

The first book I purchased as a young college student that was not required reading for a class was *Markings* by Dag Hammarskjold. His words say best what I feel with intense gratitude: "For all that has been, Thanks. For all that will be, Yes."

Lectio Divina:
A Simple Methodology

HOW TO BEGIN?

- Prepare yourself for silence. As in conversation, we need to be present to one another, so in *lectio* we prepare ourselves to be present to the voice of God.

- Sit quietly before the word of God. It is not easy; reading for meaning is an art to be practiced. Those who practice meditation are very specific about creating a posture for coming before God, with hands held open, sitting in a straight-back chair that will help you stay alert.

- As much as is possible, create a place for exterior silence. If you can, turn off technology in order to create an environment for quiet reading and listening. You may want to read aloud, so create a place where that feels comfortable.

- Focus on interior silence, what some call the silence of the mind. As you become practiced in *lectio* you will find yourself aware of the many conversations that vie for attention within. As in contemplation, some suggest that you keep a pad and pen nearby to jot a word to which you may decide to return later; it often helps remove the distraction.

THE PROCESS OF LECTIO DIVINA

1. *Lectio*: Select and read a very short passage of Scripture—just a few verses. My advice: read until something causes you to say, "Huh." It doesn't sound very sophisticated, but try it. Read a text out loud so you see, say and hear the words.

2. *Meditatio*: Meditate on a concept, idea, word or phrase that seems to stand out in the passage. Don't look necessarily for something profound or complex; it may be simple. Think about the word or idea. Reflective thought is what is called for here.

3. *Oratio*: Pray. Pray with words or silently, but enter the place of prayer seeking the presence of God. Brother Lawrence, a seventeenth-century monk spoke of "the practice of the presence of God" as perpetual prayer for awareness of God.[1]

4. *Contemplatio*: Move from prayer to the stillness of contemplation, which simply means to look at something thoughtfully for a long time. Remain in silence, listening to God. Don't be in a hurry.

People often return to the text and read it a second time and repeat the four steps again. In silence, continue to ask, "How is my life being touched by this passage?"

A third reading then moves one to ask, "What action do I need to take as a result of what I have heard?"

Transference and Countertransference

Transference is when the mentee begins to transfer feelings, positive or negative, from other people to the mentor. "The client 'transfers' to the therapist [mentor] the role of someone, usually a significant other person from the client's past, and reacts toward the therapist as if she or he were that important childhood figure."[1] This can include feelings of attraction but also, more deeply, expectations that the mentor will protect or harm, care for or abuse, love or reject them. Counter-transference is when the mentor does the same with a mentee. "If we, as guides, find ourselves between sessions spending a lot of time thinking about one particular person we are seeing, if we find ourselves in this person's presence trying to elicit praise or other positive remarks, if we worry that this person may terminate the relationship, if we dream frequently about this person, or if we try to intervene in her or his life outside the guidance session, we may be caught in what therapists call 'countertransference.'"[2] The complexity of these psychological and spiritual issues requires professional boundaries, which is what makes accountability important to the mentor. "The possibility for countertransference occurring in all guides, both male and female, provides reason enough for guides to be receiving spiritual guidance themselves."[3]

Transference can take different forms. Romantic transference is when a client develops erotic or romantic feelings for the therapist. Likewise, mentees can transfer feelings of love, affection or attraction to their mentor. We must be vigilant when physical attraction or emotional attachment enters the room. Just as therapists must pay attention to transference and countertransference, so the mentor must stay vigilant. Parental transference is common when a client develops feelings of attachment or anger as they transfer their feelings about parents to the mentor, pastor or counselor.

Countertransference can often lead to entanglement. Sometimes feelings of anger, frustration or annoyance may be stirred because a client looks, speaks, or sounds like a sibling, parent, spouse or colleague.

While these are issues often experienced by therapists and doctors, they are sometimes deflected and even ignored by those in ministry. My own training in spiritual formation addressed these issues only in a general way. Undoubtedly that is why supervision for therapists is an ongoing ethical practice. Good mentors have good mentors.

For clergy, mentoring can become an especially complicated "dual relationship" because we are both preacher and mentor. At one moment we are the one who preaches the Word in sermons or classes and in the next moment we are mentor. Confusion about role and authority may become problematic. Accountability to other clergy or our mentor is essential. Transparency about our work with others is one way we create accountable practices.

Discernment Questions
for Choosing a Mentor

☞

My colleague Walter Wright created a list of questions to assess a potential mentor. It is profoundly important because it compels the prospective mentee to explore their motivation and calibrate their expectations. It looks like a long list, but it's very wise. Whether they are all asked in an actual interview, it is useful for the mentee to consider them in order to create realistic and honest expectations. These are questions to be asked by the mentee in preparation for meeting the mentor; they may also be used as tools for an interview of the prospective mentor, but don't miss the larger point: there is a step of discernment that will lead to wise decision making for both mentor and mentee.

Why do you respect this person and the life, leadership and wisdom he models?

How accurate is her understanding of her own journey?

Who have been his mentors?

How articulately does she reflect on her life, experience and learning?

What is his philosophy or theology of management?

What has she learned lately—is she still learning and growing?

What does openness, transparency and honest speaking mean to him?
When does he listen, and when does he talk?
How is her strength of character revealed in her values and integrity?
How does he handle conflict and adversity?
What does she encourage and affirm?
Why does he believe in your potential?
How well does she understand your agenda for development?
What will being accessible mean to him?
What gives her hope?[1]

What About Differences That Might Exist Between Mentor and Mentee?

My own mentors have included clergy and laity, men and women, peers, elders, and those younger than me. Differences exist between people that deserve attention. That which may be considered barriers can also become a bridge for giving and receiving wisdom. Age and cultural and gender differences need to help shape the approach we take to the mentee, what expectations we each bring and how we proceed. Some spiritual directors will only work with their own gender. Others, because of role, are required to mentor across gender lines and to accept conversations with all who ask. Differences aren't necessarily barriers, but there is value for us in noticing and naming them.

Age

A most obvious difference is age. Generational differences are important to assess by both mentor and mentee. There are sometimes differences in language used by older and younger people. Forms of humor, use of sarcasm, what we each consider spiritual and our use of religious language are sometimes very different in our changing cultural landscape. What once was considered profane is now mainstream humor. A mentor who is unable to accept generationally different communication forms from a younger mentee may quickly alienate and shut down helpful communications. Some mentors might use biblical references freely while a mentee may be biblically illiterate. Honest inquiry is often the most direct step to take. Ask the question that is on your mind.

CULTURE

Cultural icons and forms of communication may be barriers between people. Movies, videos, songs, blogs, websites and even apps on smartphones may create communication differences between the generations. I work in a graduate school where movies and videos are commonly used as an important part of conversations. I have learned to unashamedly ask for summaries and insights into art, music and film about which I might know nothing at all. Use of social media is sometimes another barrier that exists. I do not have Facebook or Twitter accounts. In some communities, I know that is almost heresy, but I do not. But most of my mentees are active users of all forms of social media. Increasingly we need to agree to the forms of communication we'll use with each other: email, text, face time, twitter, and so on. In some of these forms, questions of confidentiality are important. If you find yourself uncertain about words, ideas, movies, painting or texts, you must ask.

Socioeconomic differences are another set of differences that can affect the communication between mentor and mentee, especially if there are major demographic differences in wealth between the two. Something as simple as housing and living arrangements are important to know. Assignments for "private and reflective time" may be impossible to create for a mentee who lives in community or in rental units or apartments. Some people live with extended families in small housing facilities. Attention to life settings is necessary.

ETHNICITY AND RACE

Ethnicity and race are also obvious differences. What is common in certain ethnic cultures may seem strange or need to be explained. I remember a student who told me that in his culture, a pastor would never sit face-to-face with a parishioner because it would feel dishonorable to the mentee. In some cultures, couples seek out counseling and mentoring together, not apart from one another. Preparation for mentoring across lines of ethnic and racial diversity may include consulting with others and reading about intercultural credibility and competency. While it is beyond the scope of this book, honest and transparent discussion from the start will set a direction or assess the ability for mentor and mentee to work well together.

GENDER

Gender is also important. Mentors will need to decide if they are willing to mentor across the gender divide or if accommodations are needed. One colleague chooses to meet in a restaurant or public place when mentoring people of the opposite gender. His policy is that his wife is informed of the mentoring he does with woman and, if the mentee is married, he will meet her husband.[1] Some choose an office with a glass door or leave the door open. Also important is awareness of spouses and their readiness for a husband or wife to engage in this work. One of the great threats to effective spiritual growth is secrecy from spouses about topics to be discussed in mentoring. In our eagerness to work with the mentee, we may forget the larger web of their families, coworkers, friends and others. One rule of thumb is to say only to the mentee in private what you are willing to say to their spouse or family in their presence. What we believe God says to the individual will not be different than what God will say about their marriage, family or work. My own practice is to encourage spouses to talk as openly as possible about the work being done in the privacy of mentoring.

Undercurrents of sexual interest or tension can be barriers. This leads many mentors to choose only to mentor someone of the same gender but for others it prompts the setting of wise boundaries and a practice of vigilant care. Accountability for mentors by peers or supervisors is one way to practice vigilance.

ROLES

For some the natural inclination is to go to a pastor for spiritual direction. He or she is known to you, has spiritual authority, and presumably training and skill. For some, that person is a youth pastor, campus pastor, discipleship leader or coach. We start there because they are the obvious choice. Often older, they carry a mantle of authority, wisdom and discernment because of the job they have or the role they play. Teachers, professors, coaches or counselors also fall into this category. Role is not relationship, however, so look beyond the role and trust your inner leanings. To whom are you led for wisdom or insights? Another way to ask the question is, who do you trust? Ultimately, the one we trust is the Holy Spirit, but Carolyn Gratton's research defines four reasons we are moved to trust in people as spiritual guides:

1. They are not totally preoccupied.

2. They adhere to a value horizon we ourselves respect. In other words, they point beyond themselves to the coherence of a trustworthy tradition.

3. There is an inner appeal that I find supportive or challenging or inspiring.

4. They treat others with transcendent respect.[2]

Relationships between mentors and mentees can become complex as vulnerable information and insights are shared. Trust can be formed and lost just as readily. Maintaining trust is a two-way street. Mentees can speak critically and inappropriately of mentors, and mentors can become untrustworthy as well. Vigilance to three things is essential. First is vigilance to the purpose. Once a covenant is created, it becomes imperative that mentors return to the purpose occasionally to remind both parties of the essential goals. Second is vigilance to place. Mentoring may take place in public but it most often is in an office behind closed doors. Most find it wise to have others present in an outer office during mentoring or for glass windows to be available in doors so there is no risk of impropriety. Third is vigilance to confidentiality. Just as pastors, counselors, attorneys and other professionals maintain confidentiality agreements, so mentors and mentees need to agree on the level of confidentiality about the work being done together.

Differences exist and can add to the curiosity we bring to the table. Most are not insurmountable barriers but require intentional conversation for them to become good bridges. Be direct and to the point. Ask the questions that you have and name the issues as your own. "I am puzzled by . . ." "I wonder if you would be willing to help me understand why . . ." "It might seem natural to you, but something is different than my experience. Can we talk about it?"

Walt Wright is wise in his caution:

At its heart, mentoring is a relationship, a caring connection between two persons. As such it is rich with possibilities for learning but also filled with risk. . . . Mentors are human beings with flaws and failings. We like to think of mentors as those who are above us, beyond us, on a pedestal, models of success. And they may well be. But they are always human beings—flawed, wounded—seeking to understand, live and contribute to life. Mentors may let you down. You may let your mentors down. Any strong relationship must carry within it the commitment to forgive and trust again if the relationship is to survive for the long haul.[3]

Notes

INTRODUCTION

[1]Cicero, *De Amicitia*, Loeb Classic Library, section 27, available at http://penelope.uchicago.edu/Thayer/E/Roman/Texts/Cicero/Laelius_de_Amicitia/text*.html.

[2]Ibid., section 2.

[3]Ibid., section 22.

[4]Eugene H. Peterson, *The Jesus Way: A Conversation on the Ways That Jesus Is the Way* (Grand Rapids: Eerdmans, 2007), 18.

[5]Thomas Kelley, *A Testament of Devotion* (New York: HarperCollins, 1996), 1.

CHAPTER ONE: READING WITH A CONSECRATED PURPOSE

[1]Samuel Langhorne Clemens, quoted online at www.ieor.berkeley.edu/~lim/twain.html.

[2]Alan Jones, *Passion for Pilgrimage* (New York: HarperCollins, 1995), 4.

[3]Lacy Clark Ellman, *Pilgrim Principles: Journeying with Intention in Everyday Life* ([US]: n.p., 2013). Lacy also blogs at asacredjourney.net.

[4]Ibid., 22.

[5]Aelred of Rivaulx, in *The Westminster Collection of Christian Quotations*, ed. Martin Manser (Louisville, KY: John Knox Press, 2001), 117.

[6]Second Corinthians 3:3, translated by N. T. Wright, quoted in N. T. Wright, *Reflecting the Glory: Meditations for Living Christ's Life in the World* (Minneapolis: Augsburg, 1998), 15, emphasis added.

[7]Henri J. M. Nouwen, *Spiritual Direction: Wisdom for the Long Walk of Faith* (New York: HarperCollins, 2006).

[8]10,000 Maniacs, "Cherry Tree," lyrics by Robert Buck and Natalie Merchant, *In My Tribe*, prod. Peter Asher (Elektra, 1987), available online at www.azlyrics.com/lyrics/10000maniacs/cherrytree.html.

[9]Tilden Edward, *Spiritual Friend: Reclaiming the Gift of Spiritual Direction* (Matwah, NJ: Paulist Press, 1980), 248.

[10]William Barry, S.J., *God's Passionate Desire* (Chicago: Loyola Press, 2008), 108.

[11]Cathy N. Davidson, *Now You See It: How the Brain Science of Attention Will Transform the Way We Live, Work, and Learn* (New York: Viking, 2011), 31.

[12]Ibid., 55.

[13]William A. Barry, S.J, *Finding God in All Things* (Notre Dame, IN: Ave Maria Press, 1991).

INTERLUDE: SPIRITUAL MENTORING AS HOSPITALITY

[1]Margaret Guenther, *Holy Listening: The Art of Spiritual Direction* (Lanham, MD: Rowman & Littlefield, 1992), 7.

[2]Henri J. M. Nouwen, *Ministry and Spirituality* (New York: Continuum, 1996), 217.

[3]Guenther, *Holy Listening*, 19.

[4]Ibid., 20.

[5]From the Rule of St. Benedict, available online at www.osb.org/rb/text/rbeaad1.html.

CHAPTER TWO: GOD AS AUTHOR

[1]Wendell Berry, *Jayber Crow, a Novel, The Life Story of Jayber Crow, Barber, of the Port William Membership, as Written by Himself* (Washington, DC: Counterpoint, 2000), 83.

[2]Ibid.

[3]Ibid., 37.

[4]Barbara Brown Taylor, *Home by Another Way* (Cambridge, MA: Cowley, 1999), 141.

[5]Jean-Pierre de Caussade, *The Sacrament of the Present Moment* (New York: Harper & Row, 1982).

[6]Keith R. Anderson and Randy D. Reese, *Spiritual Mentoring: A Guide for Seeking and Giving Direction* (Downers Grove, IL: InterVarsity Press, 1999), 95.

[7]Eugene Peterson, *Christ Plays in Ten Thousand Places* (Grand Rapids: Eerdmans, 2005), 1.

[8]Berry, *Jayber Crow*, 37-38.

[9]Ibid., 37.

[10]Richard Rohr, *Falling Upward: A Spirituality for the Two Halves of Life* (San Francisco: Jossey-Bass, 2011), 147, emphasis in original.

[11]Richard Rohr and John Feister, *Things Hidden: Scripture as Spirituality* (Cincinnati, OH: St. Anthony Messenger Press, 2008), 30.

[12]Cathy N. Davidson, *Now You See It: How the Brain Science of Attention Will Transform the Way We Live, Work, and Learn* (New York: Viking, 2011), 291.

[13]Ibid., 291.

[14]Eugene Peterson, *Working the Angles: The Shape of Pastoral Integrity* (Grand Rapids: Eerdmans, 1987), 103-4.

[15]Ibid., 103.

CHAPTER THREE: LIFE AS TEXT

[1]Richard Rohr, *Falling Upward: A Spirituality for the Two Halves of Life* (San Francisco: Jossey-Bass, 2011), 151.

[2]Francis de Sales, *Introduction to the Devout Life*, trans. John K. Ryan (New York: Doubleday-Image, 1972), introduction.

[3]Available online at www.ccel.org/bible/phillips/NoteVisitedPlanet.htm.

[4]Philip Babcock Gove, ed., *Webster's Third International Dictionary* (Springfield, MA: G. & C. Merriam, 1981), 1412.

[5]Thomas Kelley, *A Testament of Devotion* (New York: HarperCollins, 1996), 1.

[6]Keith R. Anderson, *The Spirituality of Listening: Living What You Hear* (Downers Grove, IL: InterVarsity Press, 2016), 103-4.

[7]Carolyn Gratton, *The Art of Spiritual Guidance: A Contemporary Approach to Growing in the Spirit* (New York: Crossroad, 1993), 39.

[8]Ibid., 40.

INTERLUDE: CORE CURRICULUM

[1]Liz Budd Ellman, "What Is Spiritual Direction?" Spiritual Directors International, www.sdiworld.org/find-a-spiritual-director/what-is-spiritual -direction.

[2]James Keegan, S.J., quoted at www.sdiworld.org/find-a-spiritual-director /what-is-spiritual-direction.

[3]Marian Cowan, quoted at www.sdiworld.org/find-a-spiritual-director/what -is-spiritual-direction.

CHAPTER FOUR: THE MENTOR AS COREADER

[1]Chris Bruno, *Man Maker Project: Boys Are Born, Men Are Made* (Eugene, OR: Pickwick, 2015), xxii.

[2]Ibid., 112.

[3]Henri J. M. Nouwen, *Reaching Out: The Three Movements of the Spiritual Life* (Garden City, NY: Doubleday, 1975), 8-9.

[4]Ibid., 9.

[5]Dan Allender, *To Be Told: God Invites You to Coauthor Your Future* (Colorado Springs: WaterBrook Press, 2005), 11.

[6]Ibid., 40.

INTERLUDE: STYLES OF MENTORING

[1]Gordon F. Shea, *Mentoring*, rev. ed. (Menlo Park, CA: Crisp Publications, 1997).

CHAPTER FIVE: IMPERFECT PEOPLE AS MENTORS

[1]Laura Hillenbrand, *Unbroken: A World War II Story of Survival, Resilience, and Redemption* (New York: Random House, 2014).

[2]Margaret Guenther, *Holy Listening: The Art of Spiritual Direction* (Lanham, MD: Rowman & Littlefield, 1992), xi.

[3]Richard Rohr, *Falling Upward: A Spirituality for the Two Halves of Life* (San Francisco: Jossey-Bass, 2011), 43.

[4]Ibid., 279.

[5]N. T. Wright, *Reflecting the Glory: Meditations for Living Christ's Life in the World* (Minneapolis, Augsburg, 1998), 32.

[6]Brennan Manning, *Ruthless Trust: The Ragamuffin's Path to God* (New York: HarperCollins, 2000), 11-12.

[7]"Anne Lamott Shares All That She Knows," Salon, April 10, 2015, www.salon .com/2015/04/10/anne_lamott_shares_all_that_she_knows_everyone_is _screwed_up_broken_clingy_and_scared.

[8]Eugene Peterson, *Christ Plays in Ten Thousand Places* (Grand Rapids: Eerdmans, 2005), 237.

INTERLUDE: SPIRITUAL MENTORING AS *CURA ANIMARUM*

[1]Eugene Peterson, "Curing Souls: The Forgotten Art," ChristianityToday.com, www.christianitytoday.com/le/1983/summer/83l3048.html.

[2]Source unknown.

[3]Richard Baxter, *The Reformed Pastor: A Pattern for Personal Growth and Ministry*, ed. James Houston (Vancouver: Regent College Publishing, 1985), 27.
[4]Ibid., 73-78.
[5]Ibid., 37.

INTERLUDE: SPIRITUAL MENTORING AS DISILLUSIONMENT

[1]Eric Partridge, *Origins: A Short Etymological Dictionary of Modern English* (New York: Greenwich House, 1983), 368.
[2]Barbara Brown Taylor, *God in Pain: Sermons on Suffering* (Nashville: Abingdon, 1998), 20.

CHAPTER SEVEN: WHAT DOES A MENTORING SESSION LOOK LIKE?

[1]John Steinbeck, *Travels with Charley in Search of America* (New York: Penguin, 1962), 16.
[2]Ibid.
[3]Ibid., 41.
[4]Thomas Merton, *New Seeds of Contemplation* (New York: Abbey of Gethsemani, 1961).
[5]Ibid., p. 37.
[6]Ibid.
[7]Cathy N. Davidson, *Now You See It: How the Brain Science of Attention Will Transform the Way We Live, Work, and Learn,* (New York: Viking, 2011), 171.
[8]Rule of Benedict, Prologue, 9, in Joan Chittister, OSB, *Wisdom Distilled from the Daily: Living the Rule of St. Benedict Today* (San Francisco: HarperSanFrancisco, 1990), 32.

INTERLUDE: ASKING GREAT QUESTIONS

[1]John Terpstra, *Skin Boat: Acts of Faith and Other Navigations* (Kentville, NS: Gaspereau Press, 2009), 9.
[2]Ibid.

CHAPTER EIGHT: WISDOM FOR THE LONG WALK OF FAITH

[1]Estate of Henri J. M. Nouwen, Michael J. Christensen and Rebecca Laird, *Spiritual Direction: Wisdom for the Long Walk of Faith* (New York: HarperCollins, 2006), xv.
[2]Ibid., xvi.
[3]Ibid.

[4]Cited in Vivian Giang, "What It Takes to Change Your Brain's Patterns After Age 25," *Fast Company*, April 28, 2015, www.fastcompany.com/3045424 /work-smart/what-it-takes-to-change-your-brains-patterns-after-age-25.

[5]Ibid.

[6]Ibid.

[7]Ibid.

[8]Ibid.

[9]Ibid.

[10]Ibid.

[11]Eugene Peterson, *The Pastor: A Memoir* (New York: HarperOne, 2011), 230.

[12]Carrie Newcomer, "Holy as a Day Is Spent," www.songlyrics.com/carrie -newcomer/holy-as-a-day-is-spent-lyrics. See Newcomer perform this at www.youtube.com/watch?v=2qZyoRiBteI.

[13]Frederick Buechner, *Wishful Thinking: A Theological ABC* (New York: Harper & Row, 1973), 82-83.

INTERLUDE: SPIRITUAL MENTORING AS ECOLOGY

[1]Barbara Brown Taylor, *An Altar in the World: A Geography of Faith* (New York: HarperOne, 2009).

[2]Quoted in David Naugle, "Introduction to Kuyper's Thought" The Kuyperian blog (February 2001), http://kuyperian.blogspot.com/2004/08/introduction -to-kuypers-thought.html.

CHAPTER NINE: CREATING THE PACE

[1]Steve Zeitlin, *Because God Loves Stores: An Anthology of Jewish Storytelling* (New York: Crossroad, 1997), 7.

[2]St. Aelred of Rivaulx, *Spiritual Friendship* (Kalamazoo, MI: Cistercian, 1977), book 1, #1, p. 51.

[3]Brennan Manning, *Ruthless Trust: The Ragamuffin's Path to God* (New York: HarperCollins, 2000), 24-25.

[4]Cathy N. Davidson, *Now You See It: How the Brain Science of Attention Will Transform the Way We Live, Work, and Learn* (New York: Viking, 2011), 41.

[5]Ibid., 55, emphasis added.

[6]Ibid., 56.

INTERLUDE: SPIRITUAL MENTORING AS PRAYER

[1]Richard Foster, *Prayer: Finding the Heart's True Home* (New York: Harper-Collins, 1992), vii-viii, xiii.

[2]Ibid., 1.

CHAPTER TEN: SUSTAINING MOMENTUM THROUGH ACCOUNTABILITY

[1]Keith R. Anderson and Randy D. Reese, *Spiritual Mentoring: A Guide for Seeking and Giving Direction* (Downers Grove, IL: InterVarsity Press, 1999), 126.

[2]T. S. Eliot, "Ash Wednesday," in T. S. Eliot, *Collected Poems 1909–1962* (London: Faber and Faber, 1963). Available online at www.msgr.ca/msgr-7/ash_wednesday_t_s_eliot.htm.

[3]N. T. Wright, "The Bible and Christian Imagination." *Response*, www.spu.edu/depts/uc/response/summer2k5/features/imagination.asp.

[4]"The Daily Examen," accessed on January 4, 2016, at www.ignatianspirituality.com/ignatian-prayer/the-examen.

[5]See the Book of Common Prayer online at www.bcponline.org.

[6]Ignatius, quoted in William A. Barry, SJ, *Finding God in All Things* (Notre Dame, IN: Ave Maria Press, 1991), 13-14.

[7]See "Making the Full Spiritual Exercises," accessed January 4, 2016, https://www.manresa-sj.org/235_Full_SPEX-2.htm.

INTERLUDE: SPIRITUAL MENTORING AS GEOGRAPHY

[1]Kathleen Norris, *Dakota: A Spiritual Geography* (New York: Houghton Mifflin, 2001).

[2]Description found at www.amazon.com/Dakota-Spiritual-Geography-Kathleen-Norris/dp/0618127240.

[3]Margaret Guenther, *Holy Listening: The Art of Spiritual Direction* (Lanham, MD: Rowman & Littlefield, 1992), 71.

CHAPTER ELEVEN: ENDING WELL

[1]Wendell Berry, *Jayber Crow, a Novel, The Life Story of Jayber Crow, Barber, of the Port William Membership, as Written by Himself* (Washington, DC: Counterpoint, 2000), 54.

[2]William James, "The Will to Believe," available online at www.bartleby.com/97/425.html.

[3]Berry, *Jayber Crow*, 132.

INTERLUDE: TEN ESSENTIALS FOR THE MENTOR'S LIBRARY

[1]Jeff Bowman, "How to: Packing the Ten Essentials," The Mountaineers, February 25, 2014, www.mountaineers.org/learn/how-to/the-ten-essentials.

[2]Eugene Peterson, *The Pastor: A Memoir* (New York: HarperOne, 2011), 230.

Appendix One: *Lectio Divina*

[1]Brother Lawrence, *The Practice of the Presence of God*, available online at www
.ccel.org/ccel/lawrence/practice.

Appendix Two: Transference and Countertransference

[1]Carolyn Gratton, *The Art of Spiritual Guidance* (New York: Crossroad, 1993),
88.
[2]Ibid., 89.
[3]Ibid.

Appendix Three: Discernment Questions
for Choosing a Mentor

[1]Walter C. Wright, *Mentoring: The Promise of Relational Leadership* (Bletchley,
UK: Paternoster, 2004), 70.

Appendix Four: What About Differences That
Might Exist Between Mentor and Mentee?

[1]Walter Wright, *Mentoring: The Promise of Relational Leadership* (Bletchley,
UK: Paternoster, 2006), 99.
[2]Carolyn Gratton, *The Art of Spiritual Guidance* (New York: Crossroad, 1993),
112-13.
[3]Walter C. Wright, *Mentoring: The Promise of Relational Leadership* (Eugene,
OR: Wipf & Stock, 2013), 66-67.

Also by Keith R. Anderson

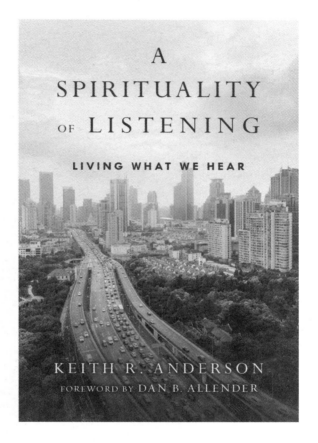

A Spirituality of Listening:
Living What We Hear
978-0-8308-4609-2

formatio
TRADITION. EXPERIENCE.
TRANSFORMATION.

Formatio books from InterVarsity Press follow the rich tradition of the church in the journey of spiritual formation. These books are not merely about being informed, but about being transformed by Christ and conformed to his image. Formatio stands in InterVarsity Press's evangelical publishing tradition by integrating God's Word with spiritual practice and by prompting readers to move from inward change to outward witness. InterVarsity Press uses the chambered nautilus for Formatio, a symbol of spiritual formation because of its continual spiral journey outward as it moves from its center. We believe that each of us is made with a deep desire to be in God's presence. Formatio books help us to fulfill our deepest desires and to become our true selves in light of God's grace.